APPLYING
FOR
RESEARCH
FUNDING

WITHDRAWN

Joanne B. Ries
Carl G. Leukefeld

APPLYING
FOR
RESEARCH
FUNDING

Getting
Started
and
Getting
Funded

SAGE Publications
International Educational and Professional Publisher
Thousand Oaks   London   New Delhi

For information address:

 SAGE Publications, Inc.
2455 Teller Road
Thousand Oaks, California 91320
E-mail: order@sagepub.com

SAGE Publications Ltd.
6 Bonhill Street
London EC2A 4PU
United Kingdom

SAGE Publications India Pvt. Ltd.
M-32 Market
Greater Kailash I
New Delhi 110 048 India

Printed in the United States of America

Library of Congress Cataloging-in-Publication Data

Ries, Joanne B.
    Applying for research funding: Getting started and getting funded.
  / Joanne B.. Ries, Carl G. Leukefeld.
        p. cm.
    Includes bibliographical references and index.
    ISBN 0-8039-5364-X.—ISBN 0-8039-5365-8 (pbk.)
    1. Research grants. 2. Grants-in-aid. 3. Proposal writing for
grants. I. Leukefeld, Carl G.   II. Title.
    HG177.R53   1995   94-35077
    658.15'224—dc20

              98 99 10 9   8   7   6   5   4   3

Sage Production Editor: Astrid Virding

Contents

Preface

Comprehending the funding process has frequently taken years for many successfully funded researchers and others with funded projects. To understand the grant and contract application process and consistently be competitive for either foundation or governmental sources are the thrusts of this volume. For the authors, those years passed in two very different ways and environments. Joanne spent that time at the University of Kentucky working with a variety of persons by helping them develop funded grant and contract applications. Her wide experience in seeking funded research has ranged from private foundations to multiple governmental agencies. During that same period of time, Carl was with the Public Health Service in a variety of roles related to grant and contract projects for research, services, and training from the funding perspective.

It was natural after we met—when Carl joined the University of Kentucky faculty—that during discussions over coffee and at other times, we soon learned that our thoughts about preparing competitive grant and contract applications and getting funded were surprisingly similar, although frequently for very different reasons. After preparing a paper together on funding strategies, we learned that we had made multiple presentations about getting funded and had talked with many others about getting funded. We also discovered that we were discussing detailed strategies we had found to be successful and wondered why others did not use them.

We really can't remember when we came to the conclusion that we should do a book about getting funded. But before we reached that conclusion and took ourselves too seriously, we did a literature search and critically examined what we might be able to add to the literature. We discovered that the kinds of "coaching" both of us had been doing with the systemic approach we had applied was not available in the literature. So that's how this volume was developed with a focus on helping the new as well as the seasoned investigator become most successful in obtaining external funding. Some of our colleagues may say that we assembled our notes; to some extent that is true, but we have added a great deal more.

We need to clarify the purpose of this book. That clarification is related to the structured coaching that follows—it is a beginning for applying successful approaches for some and for others it will hopefully sharpen what is already known. We have not attempted to completely cover all eventualities and details related to obtaining and competing for funding. We have focused on strategies for developing a competitive application because we recognize that things change and funding streams shift. We can't stress enough that contacting the funding source, obtaining the most current guidelines, and strictly following those guidelines are very, very important for success.

In assuming the role of coach, we have made several assumptions that may not be reasonable for everyone. However, we believe that we have presented the assumptions so that the reader will be able to understand our emphases and to critically judge them accordingly. We also have repeated important points throughout the chapters so the reader will not have to start at the beginning each time but can pick up the book and browse without the need for backward or forward reading. Frankly, we are not sure how well we did this and look forward to feedback and comments.

Coaching can be difficult to accept because it is repetitive and includes basic information that is elementary for some individuals. Our purpose is to provide guidance based on what we have found to be successful for a variety of persons and a variety of funding sources. Although there are always exceptions, we have concentrated on mainstream competitive grant and contract applications. We use the Public Health Service and grants from the National Institutes of Health (NIH) as the models for discussing grant funding and related activities including peer review. For us, the NIH system is the process with which we have had the most experience, and we believe that it is most representative of other application submission and review systems.

We would also like to underscore the fact that this is not an idea book, but it is to be used after an idea is formulated. Keep in mind that there is nothing like good science or good project programming in order to be successful in obtaining funding. But a good idea and good science if not presented in a logical, understandable, and compelling manner will not be successful. So there needs to be balance between science and presentation, coupled with commitment and perseverance.

Finally, each of us have had discussions with a variety of investigators and those aspiring to become investigators. We have learned that becoming competitive and funded has been a character-building series of events for many and continues to be a daily experience for us. We would, therefore, like to thank our families, and particularly our children for bearing with us during our journey of preparing this volume. They have provided support, asked questions, and provided guidance that some of us might consider to be coaching.

1

Introduction

This book was developed to provide guidance for the new investigator and others interested in competing for grant and contract funds. Observations indicate that more and more, community agency practitioners and university and college faculty in clinical and basic science departments are being shoved to the application submission starting line earlier and earlier in their careers. Competing successfully for national funding and the benefits of securing external funding in an environment of shrinking resources are important career markers.

As authors, we did not jump into developing this book; rather it developed gradually over years of consultation and advice giving, both separately and together. In our search for consulting resources we found several books on the grant process, but nothing met our needs. So what follows is a synthesis of notes and discussions describing a method for systematically approaching the application process and developing a competitive application. This is not a "how to get a research idea" book, but a book that focuses on structuring an idea to develop a competitive application. We hope that it will meet the needs of the new investigator who is poised at the starting line and ready to begin, and others who wish to continue their research career.

Topics are presented in seven areas with the repetition we believe necessary so that a busy person can use each chapter separately and not waste time paging through other chapters. Part I presents the important components of making choices in getting started in preparing the application. Part II discusses key contacts that we have found useful in developing competitive applications. Part III presents the strengths and weaknesses of various research environments. Part IV presents what to include and when to write an application, while Part V gives practical suggestions on writing persuasive applications. Part VI contains suggestions for focusing on the reviewers as the target for the successful application. Finally, Part VII provides suggestions related to what happens when an application is funded and what happens when it is not funded.

PART I. MAJOR COMPONENTS: GETTING STARTED

The goal of Part I is to describe what we have found to be the ingredients of a competitive research application. The ingredients are distributed across three areas—the investigator, the application materials, and the funding mechanisms.

The first decision to be made is whether a potential investigator has credentials valued by funding sources. Chapter 2 provides an inventory of information and skills for a principal investigator. The inventory includes academic training, technical and research skills, management skills, and the relationship of the investigator's location to funding opportunities. In addition, we describe the ideal profile of a principal investigator and offer suggestions for filling in professional gaps.

Every application, whether it be for private or government funding, must contain certain basic components. The Public Health Service application was chosen as a guide throughout this book because it includes many of the possible application components. It provides detailed instructions, ranging from the general appearance of the application to what should be included in the project plan. In our opinion, it is a useful model. Chapter 3 describes the appearance of the competitive application and presents expectations. Reviewers' expectations are derived from the mission statement of the funding source and from the application instructions (e.g., number of pages, size of type, order of information, kinds of information, number of copies, and other miscellaneous items) reflecting features important to the funding source and to the subsequent funding decision-making process. This chapter also briefly describes the structure of the project plan and the need for it to meet the expectations set by the principal investigator. We emphasize the importance of an organizing principle that will lead the reviewers to agree with the principal investigator's judgment about the need for the research.

Chapter 4 describes selected funding mechanisms used predominantly by agencies and universities. The choice of the funding mechanism is important and influences success. The funding mechanism selected should be appropriate for the experience, career status, and positioning of the principal investigator. The variety of mechanisms and special applications provides options for investigators in diverse career paths and locations.

PART II. KEY CONNECTIONS: OPENING MOVES

Part II focuses on key connections that can facilitate the successful completion of a grant application. Chapters 5 and 6 describe the formal and informal resources that should be used.

It has been our experience that the more use an individual makes of available resources, the easier it is to prepare an application. Chapters 5 and 6 discuss how resources can be beneficial to an investigator and emphasize the need for developing and maintaining open communication channels with others in respect to using these resources.

Chapter 7 is concerned with how one uses the information provided by funding sources to select a funding source best suited to the proposed project. The chapter also includes a brief discussion of how to use funding source guidelines to develop a competitive application. Whether gain can be achieved by submitting an application to a source not interested in the project is questionable; submitting an application that does not follow the rules of the funding source is foolish.

Funding sources invest in projects according to priorities and preferred topics, the amount of funds available, and the timeframes for the projects. It is desirable that the requirements of applicant and funding source match. Chapter 7 also presents considerations in choosing a research topic, an explanation of how to use positioning to determine possible funding sources, and a brief application work plan to use for meeting funding source deadlines.

The funding source provides instructions designed to facilitate the fund-ing-decision process. Therefore, it is in the principal investigator's best interest to follow these instructions as closely as possible. Thus Chapter 7 gives examples of instructions, explains where they are found, and describes what to do when instructions cannot be followed.

PART III. RESEARCH IN THE REAL WORLD:
THE PLAYING BOARD

Research environments and investigators' credentials vary. The principal investigator's credentials and the research environment must be able to support the proposed project. Therefore, different environments are better for some types of projects than others. The elements that come into play in these decisions are considered in Chapter 8.

Chapter 9 delves into the complicated and complex area of relationships. Frequently, preparing a project application requires reaching outside the immediate work and social environment of the principal investigator. Ac-cepted behavior, along with conversational and professional style, are not common across environments. For example, what is acceptable in an aca-demic environment may be a focus for criticism in a business or clinical environment. This chapter discusses the importance of being aware of differences that might exist between an investigator's host environment and a collaborator's environment.

PART IV. WHAT AND WHEN TO WRITE:
RULES OF THE GAME

Part IV is devoted to outlining, in detail, *what* is to be included in an application. Principal investigators using identical application materials can easily submit applications that include different kinds of information. This chapter emphasizes the importance of making the extra effort to submit an application that attends to all available instructions.

Chapter 10 describes the research details that a reviewer will expect and the kinds of information that signal research expertise, ability, and compe-tence. Chapter 10 discusses each part of the research application research plan (e.g., title, abstract, objectives, literature review, preliminary studies or pilot work, experimental design and methods, research timeline, and human or animal subject protection issues).

Applications almost always include supporting documentation. Chapter 11 discusses this documentation. These application pages are often called "forms" and are treated with little respect. However, they are not "forms" in the usual sense of the word: They are designed to include pertinent information about the investigator and the project that the funding source has deemed necessary. This detailed information, then, provides an investigator with an opportunity to positively influence funding. Therefore, the chapter includes detailed information about biographical material, resources and environment information, other research support, literature citations, appendices, and budget. Not all funding sources require extensive information in all of these areas, but requests for some information in each of these categories are customary.

Chapter 12 describes a plan for organizing activities in order to complete the application. This plan, or timetable, and the various purposes it can serve are presented and described. In our experience, an important function of the timetable is to help the procrastinator move forward with developing an application.

PART V. HOW TO WRITE: UNIQUE MOVES

To be competitive, it is imperative that a grant application be persuasive. We believe that a host of ingredients result in a persuasive document. Part V focuses on *how* the application is written.

Chapter 13, "Writing to Be Competitive," discusses how the structure of a project plan can be used to an investigator's advantage. The chapter discusses the *language* used in a proposal and the importance of efficient, precise, and effective communication with the reviewers.

PART VI. CHECKING FOR INFRACTIONS: PREPARING FOR THE AUDIENCE

The entire application must be written with the review in mind, whether the application will be reviewed by an individual or a group. Chapter 14 discusses the facets of the review process that overshadow what is written and how it is written. The relationship of the reviewers to the funding source, as well as the organization of the reviewers, provides a filter through which each reviewer reads the application. The process governing the reviewers' actions, their everyday lives, and their professional experiences produce biases that are not overcome during the application review process. A competitive application anticipates the reviewers' reactions to an application. To this end, Chapter 14 includes a checklist that can be used to determine how well the application will meet the review committee's expectations.

PART VII. THE REVIEWERS' DECISION: ENDGAME

The reviewers' decision, in the broadest terms, falls into one of two categories—funded or not funded. In most instances an investigator anticipates the consequences of not being funded far more accurately than those of being funded. One of the most surprising revelations for many newly funded investigators is the need to wear yet another hat—that of a small business manager. Chapter 15 discusses the dimensions of a project that become activated when that yearned-for word "FUNDED" is pronounced. Chapter 16 is a discussion about the consequences of the project not being funded. When this is the situation, several options are open to the investigator(s), and guidance on how to sort through these options to determine what is most advantageous for the investigator is presented.

PART I

Major Components

Getting Started

2

The Principal Investigator

The focus of this chapter is the new investigator who wants to become an extramurally funded principal investigator (PI). A new investigator is defined here as an investigator who has not previously received external (extramural) foundation or governmental funding. If the new investigators of today are to obtain extramural funding, they must position themselves differently from PIs of previous years. In fact, we suggest that the new investigator of today cannot copy the career patterns and role models of long-term extramurally funded researchers.

We believe that to develop a competitive application and obtain extramural funding, a different personal and professional strategy is now required. In the past, those who received funding were likely to be full professors, if in academia, or directors, if in a community agency. In academia they were well established. Before their research was funded they were well-published and often well-known, at least within their disciplines and areas of research interest. Community agency staff were viewed as experts. They were respected for their knowledge and their ability to put that knowledge into practice, research, or community programming. Furthermore, the success of these principal investigators seemed to be the result of independent efforts. It appeared, and often was the case, that these investigators themselves had all the necessary information and expertise.

New and aspiring investigators respected and admired these scientists and practitioners and often believed it was presumptuous or arrogant to assume that they could also obtain external funding for their own work. Those established scientists and practitioners, as well as those with extramural funding today, give the impression that it is easy to get funding—an impression commonly made by those who have become experts. Those who are funded frequently do not talk about the help they received to locate a funding source or the bureaucratic hoops they jumped through because these activities are viewed in retrospect as inevitable parts of the process to achieve their goal. As clearing and plowing a field is not visible in the corn, the groundwork of funded research—the small research projects, the hours of literature review, the reliance on others for information about rules and regulations of funding sources as well as for scientific expertise—is not visible in the funded project. We believe that the groundwork remains essentially the same today as in the past. What does not remain the same is career pattern. Professionals are being pushed to the application submission playing board early in their careers. Seeking external funding has become an expected activity for professionals seeking recognition and promotion and it is, therefore, neither presumptuous nor arrogant for a new investigator to seek it.

The less experienced investigator is also being encouraged to become part of the external research funding industry through the creation of special programs. The new investigator is eligible for external funding for individual-initiated research projects. For example, the federal government has research funding opportunities directed specifically at the less experienced investigator (FIRST Award), as does the National Science Foundation with its Junior Faculty Research Award. These opportunities permit new investigators to be competitive for research funding because they are not penalized for their junior status. This is good news for the new investigator.

However, with the availability of funds for new investigators comes the linking of external funding to promotion in both clinical and research settings. Since the late 1970s, it has been imperative for younger professionals, such as basic scientists and selected clinicians, to get extramural research funding. In our opinion, career paths now have two new requirements: First, professionals are expected to have funded research or evaluation projects early in their careers. Second, academics who did not consider research (much less externally funded research) important to their professional progress now find it to be an integral part of their advancement and promotion. Thus it is important for these professionals to be comfortable with research or evaluation, the project application process, and grantsmanship. This comfort, in our opinion, must be coupled with expertise in a recognized topical area in which an individual can develop competence with persistent confidence.

We believe that competence is achieved through experience and the development of skills and strategies in at least three areas:

1. *Research or evaluation expertise,* which enables posing of focused and compelling questions about research and evaluation and related designs or approaches.
2. *Exquisite positioning,* which is achieved through informed networking and collaboration. Informed networking and research or evaluation collaboration provide open channels for communication within an organizational or community infrastructure, enabling appropriate choices of collaborators who can provide guidance to successful and productive professional experiences.
3. *Personal and management skills,* which are achieved through experience and practice. These skills enable the investigator to achieve peak performance, maintain good humor, and be a source of emotional and professional support for all others working on the project.

We believe that each of these three areas is critical. Achievement of excellence may not be possible in all areas, but some accomplishment in each is required. The following is an example of how neglect in the personal and management skills area could have an adverse effect on a project application:

A university-based new investigator has a great research idea, a straightforward design for testing the hypotheses, and a collaborator to cover one of the critical areas of expertise. This looks like the birth of a competitive proposal. However, during the process of completing the application, other responsibilities sidetrack the aspiring investigators. They take short cuts to get the application materials together and barely meet the deadline even after delegating the responsibility for finishing the application to the newest unit secretary.

This application will probably not be competitive. In fact, it might not make it through the preliminary checks on length requirements and completeness of supporting material. The ingredient missing from the application preparation is attention to the personal skills and strategies necessary for bringing an application to its developmental peak. The principle we would like to stress here is this: Scientific knowledge, collaboration, and personal and management skills are all needed to complete and submit a competitive application.

RESEARCH OR EVALUATION EXPERIENCE

Appraising where you are in your career with respect to your areas of research and evaluation expertise, positioning, personal skills, management skills, and strategies can be most useful in helping to plan your career. Your resume and preparatory course work reveal where you are in developing your research expertise.

High-quality research is the bedrock of a competitive proposal. Funding agencies and review groups are interested in funding and promoting good science and practice. High-quality research should contribute to the scientific information base and to the effective use of scientific and practice information that will lead to improvements in the human condition.

There is no substitute for documented research experience and formal course work in research and evaluation design and statistical methods. The successful investigator will have been a co-investigator on research or evaluation projects, either funded or nonfunded. He or she will also know something about the kinds of designs that are successful in the area of interest or about the most practical community approach. In addition, the successful investigator will have written several scientific reports and journal articles. Finally, he or she will have had enough experience with statistical methods and concepts to be able to critique statistical sections of papers in the area of interest and interpret statistical results provided by a statistical consultant.

Research or Evaluation Strengths

We developed the Research Strengths Inventory, presented in Table 2.1, to provide a realistic description of research strengths. We believe that strengths and opportunities for growth can be promoted by collecting information in several areas. Using this information, individual strengths can be identified, and areas that need strengthening can be bolstered with collaboration and mentoring. Obtaining your personal profile is easy. Read each item and check either the "yes" or the "no" column; then calculate your score according to the directions that appear after the inventory.

Table 2.1 Research Strengths Inventory

Activity	Yes	No
RESEARCH EXPERIENCE		
1. Publications		
First author research paper	_____	_____
First author research review article	_____	_____
First author research abstract	_____	_____
Other author research paper	_____	_____
Other author research review article	_____	_____
Other author research abstract	_____	_____
SCORE _____		
2. Research review function		
Peer reviewer	_____	_____
Internal research review	_____	_____
Human/animal subject committees	_____	_____
Dissertation committees	_____	_____
Regular federal reviewer	_____	_____
Ad hoc federal reviewer	_____	_____
SCORE _____		
3. Collaboration/consultation		
Collaboration initiator	_____	_____
Invited to collaborate	_____	_____
Research or evaluation design consultant	_____	_____
Statistical design consultant	_____	_____
Research methods consultant	_____	_____
Content area consultant	_____	_____
SCORE _____		
4. Research methods of previous work		
Basic research	_____	_____
Applied research	_____	_____
Evaluation research	_____	_____
Single case studies	_____	_____
Survey research	_____	_____
Experimental designs	_____	_____
SCORE _____		
5. Formal courses		
Research or evaluation design	_____	_____
Statistics	_____	_____
Qualitative methods	_____	_____
Laboratory bench work	_____	_____
Theory	_____	_____
Methods	_____	_____
SCORE _____		

continued

Table 2.1 Continued

Activity	Yes	No
6. Research hypotheses considerations		
In your interest area/outside training	_____	_____
In your research area/outside interests	_____	_____
Using methods with which you are familiar	_____	_____
Using statistics with which you are familiar	_____	_____
Availability of subjects known	_____	_____
Feasible research designs appropriate	_____	_____
SCORE _____		
7. Pilot data		
Published research	_____	_____
Two or more pilot studies completed	_____	_____
Nonpublished analyzed data	_____	_____
Nonpublished preliminary data	_____	_____
Instruments pretested successfully	_____	_____
Methods pretested successfully	_____	_____
SCORE _____		
8. Mentoring		
Available in area of methodology	_____	_____
Available in area of content	_____	_____
Available as editor	_____	_____
Ongoing in area of methodology	_____	_____
Ongoing in area of content	_____	_____
Ongoing as editor	_____	_____
SCORE _____		
POSITIONING		
9. Infrastructure—Do you know where to contact:		
An Internal Review Board	_____	_____
A research grant development office	_____	_____
Statistical consultant(s)	_____	_____
Research or evaluation consultant(s)	_____	_____
Federal research grant personnel	_____	_____
Your financial grant manager	_____	_____
SCORE _____		
PERSONAL STYLE		
10. Management Skills		
Administered a budget	_____	_____
Hired staff	_____	_____
Supervised staff	_____	_____
Chaired a research committee	_____	_____
Developed a new committee	_____	_____
Directed data collection procedures	_____	_____
SCORE _____		

Table 2.2 Research Strengths Inventory Scores

Activity	0	1	2	3	4	5	6
1. Publications							
2. Research review function							
3. Collaboration/consultation							
4. Research methods of previous work							
5. Formal courses							
6. Research hypotheses considerations							
7. Pilot data							
8. Mentoring							
9. Infrastructure							
10. Management skills							

Scoring the Research Strengths Inventory

The Research Strengths Inventory scoring scheme is as follows: 1 for yes and 0 for no. For each of the 10 activities, the maximum value is 6 and the minimum value is 0. Enter the sum for each section in the space labeled SCORE; then enter a dot in the appropriate row and column for each section's SCORE in Table 2.2, and connect the dots with a continuous line.

This personal inventory, in addition to outlining research or evaluation expertise, provides information about your funding eligibility. For example, this inventory might lead to the conclusion that an appropriate plan of action is to postpone developing a research or evaluation application. This could be the best decision if you lack community experience or have a preponderance of "nos" in the areas directly related to your ability to design and complete a research or evaluation project. If you have never, for instance, designed and completed a research project, then your first step to becoming an externally funded investigator is to do research or evaluation. If you have no publications, then a first step toward becoming an externally funded investigator is to publish so that the resulting publications can be listed on your resume. If you have research publications but think that you are weak in your experience with design and statistical methods, you probably can proceed with your proposal plans, but we suggest that you get design and statistical help.

Table 2.3 Profile of Research Strengths

Activity	Score						
	0	1	2	3	4	5	6
1. Publications				•			
2. Research review function				•			
3. Collaboration/consultation				•			
4. Research methods of previous work					•		
5. Formal courses					•		
6. Research hypotheses considerations					•		
7. Pilot data			•				
8. Mentoring				•			
9. Infrastructure		•					
10. Management skills		•					

Interpreting Your Score

If you have a vertical line in the 6 column, continue with your plans for submitting a research application. If you have a vertical line in the 0 column, reassess your research application aspirations. An example of a profile for a new investigator with sufficient credentials to submit an application is presented in Table 2.3.

From our point of view, it is important that new investigators neither underestimate nor overestimate their research or evaluation training and ability. The most likely direction is to underestimate research or evaluation backgrounds and abilities and to exaggerate the importance of deficiencies or difficulties. For example, some new investigators have discovered that forming testable hypotheses is a very difficult task. Such a person might think, "How can I submit a competitive research proposal when I find it so difficult to do one of the most basic things—form a testable hypothesis?" This is only one of the many issues that can be resolved by working with colleagues and collaborators. The important principle here is not to let your emotions get control of the decision-making process. Be as objective as you can in reviewing available data. In addition, we suggest that you ask others to look at the data. With this help, you should be able to come to a realistic conclusion about your ability to design and develop focused research or evaluation studies.

Research or Evaluation Interests

In our experience, a project application must be tightly focused on an area of science or community practice that is of interest to both the PI *and* the funding source. The important word in the previous sentence is *and*. Although this may sound like a foregone conclusion, investigators regularly submit applications in areas outside their interests.

It is important for the new investigator to establish areas of research or evaluation interest. These are the areas in which the new investigator has sufficient knowledge and experience to be able to formulate new and interesting questions or interventional solutions. These are the areas in which critical thinking is achieved and in which she or he wants to develop and expand knowledge. These are also the scientific areas exciting to the investigator.

The process of developing an area can begin by identifying your greatest interest and greatest strength. The following are some suggested activities that can help.

- A careful review of your previous publications, collaborations, and seminar presentations is a good place to start ferreting out your interest areas.
- Develop a list of your research or evaluation interests. This list should incorporate available resources and be as detailed as possible. You might use an outline format. For example, a major heading might be drug abuse, and subheadings could be, drug abuse among teenagers, the elderly, and professionals; alcohol; cocaine; experimental designs; survey designs; and qualitative research. It is critical that you explicate a picture of your interests and your preferred method of developing and testing hypotheses. What you have been doing is probably what you do best.
- Review publications from funding sources. Funding sources regularly publicize areas of interest in mission statements, lists of categories of needed research, and program announcements. It is very important that the proposed research be within the interests expressed by the funding source. However, our overall experience has been that investigators who only follow the interests of funding sources without considering their own scientific or practice interests have difficulty in preparing a competitive application because their passion is not engaged.

POSITIONING

Professional Environment

The kind of research or evaluation you can do, regardless of your interests, is largely a function of your professional and geographical environment. A project that is possible for someone in a service agency may not be possible for someone in a research university. On the other hand, a design requiring high-level, on-site technology may not be possible for a new investigator in a service agency but feasible for an investigator at a research university. Project possibilities are, therefore, restricted by the mission and structure of the submitting organization.

The following are examples of the kinds of infrastructure support we believe are important in developing competitive project applications:

- Training opportunities for new investigators
- Clinical and scientific consultation, both internal and external
- Biostatistical and database management services
- Equipment and research instruments
- Research technicians and assistants
- Support staff
- Developmental, feasibility, or pilot study opportunities

Collegial Support

An important positioning consideration is collegial support. How do your interests fit with those of your colleagues? A principle to keep in mind here is that funded research or evaluation is rarely an individual effort. Co-investigators and consultants are needed for most applications. Does your environment provide these kinds of resources, or are they available to you through collaboration with other organizations? For example, if you are located in a service organization, do you have relationships with colleagues at a research university that will enable you to use research university resources? Although it is undoubtedly easier to work with people you know and with whom you have had previous collaborations, your project might require an expertise outside that of your usual collaborators. We suggest that you talk with colleagues about research or evaluation possibilities, their project experiences, and their collaboration experiences. Although each colleague will impose a personality on any interaction, scenarios of failed collaborations that involve the same people must not be ignored. What you are trying to do in these conversations is to obtain an impression of the environment where you will be conducting your project. An unfavorable environment does not mean you cannot pursue a project. It does mean, however, that you will have to try to develop strategies and systems that transform that environment into a favorable one, because projects cannot be carried out successfully in unfavorable environments.

PERSONAL CHARACTERISTICS

Adele Scheele, in her book *Skills for Success* (1979), categorizes people as sustainers and achievers. Achievers experience different life circumstances than do sustainers. The differences, as you might guess, arise primarily from the assertiveness inherent in moving forward in a career and uncovering new information. Some of the achiever characteristics cited by Scheele are the following: a) amenability to a variety of experiences, an ability to tolerate change, and an understanding that setbacks are not failures but stepping stones to final success; b) tolerance for linking with many people, thereby increasing exposure to information and also advertising expertise; and c) a demonstration of "belonging," which means responsibility for the success of a particular project is accepted and, therefore, no associated task is considered too menial. These are all characteristics that can be developed and used profitably by a principal investigator.

The successful development and completion of a project application and the funded research project depends upon the ability to envision the total endeavor. The vision comprises the snail-paced start, the myriad of details—both projected and expected—and finally the mailing of the application. This overview can include periodic assessments of previous work, the current situation, and future probabilities. If you have not done such an assessment, helpful tools are available; an important one, we believe, is the project application timetable that we discuss in Chapter 12.

Each time an individual develops a project application, or, for that matter, any research or evaluation project, both new and familiar situations arise requiring thought and strategy development to achieve the preferred outcome. While developing an application, investigators will find situations similar to those faced during the conduct of research. However, the investigator who has completed one application faces identical situations in subsequent applications, because an application is a system of interrelated parts and each developmental stage has its unique requirements and problems. The following are situations that could arise and for which a new investigator needs to be prepared.

Barriers. A successful PI expects to encounter barriers and to surmount them. In our experience, probably no research project is envisioned, initiated, and completed without overcoming barriers. The barriers might be administrative, such as distribution of secretarial time; professional, such as a key individual planning a sabbatical; or monetary, such as a project funding cap or shortage of internal funds for pilot studies.

Control. The application process is an exercise in taking and yielding control. A successful PI can separate those aspects that he or she can control from those aspects that others (the funding source, co-investigators, secretarial help) control. Within any application for project funding, there are numerous instances where a PI must yield control to the funding source because the application process or the administrative regulations of the applicant organization demand it.

Planning. Anyone who engages in research has experience with organizing and conducting activities in an orderly manner. Developing plans in a deductive manner enables a PI to arrange the application tasks in a hierarchical order permitting each succeeding task to rest on that which came before. The result of this arrangement is a system of subgoals and intermediate goals culminating in the final goal of mailing the application. It is important to recognize the need for developing an organization system as well as the need for remaining flexible about the system.

Preparation. A PI understands the need for preparation and considers preparation time an excellent investment.

Tools. Everyone engaged in preparing an application has particular expertise or particular tools of the trade. The PI must be able to engage actively in discussions and choices about using the most preferred tools, whether they be methodology, statistics, subject selection, word processing, or the electronic highway.

Persistence. Everyone engaged in preparing an application also has other activities. The PI must be able to actively support persistence in the face of conflicting obligations and difficulties about project elements.

Self-Confidence. Self-confidence is an important element of success in any endeavor. A PI must be able to nurture her or his own self-confidence and also support that of the others developing the application.

Procrastination. A PI understands that to some extent, everyone is a procrastinator, and also that sometimes procrastination is the best action. Strategies, therefore, need to be built into the application preparation process so that forward movement is maintained when procrastination threatens to stop it. At the same time, assessment methods need to be developed to differentiate between procrastination as a barrier and procrastination as a signal that prior steps have not been completed. All systems need to be plugged in before they will operate.

Communication. A PI is comfortable with promoting and using an open communication system among those developing the application.

Resource Use. A PI knows how to seek help and advice and recognizes when it is needed. A successful PI understands that an integral part of developing a project application is building information and resource networks. Today he or she is asking for information, and tomorrow he or she will be providing it.

Decisions. A successful PI understands there are no small decisions. Each decision is a node in the net of the final application; thus, each decision has the potential for changing more than one element and, therefore, possibly influencing the funding decision.

In summary, a PI has sufficient training in the area of interest to design and conduct the project either alone or with co-investigators. The PI recognizes when other expertise is required and seeks it as appropriate. He or she is able to step out and risk getting involved with new people and new information channels. The PI is able to develop a plan and be persistent in completing the plan. Setbacks are not signals to retreat, but rather signals to reassess so that forward movement can be re-established. The PI is willing to learn and is able to conform to requests when conforming is important to the completion of a competitive application.

ACTION STRATEGIES

The following action strategies are presented to help the new investigator achieve the expectations that have been presented in this chapter.

Research or Evaluation Experience

Research or evaluation experience can be acquired in a variety of ways. Whenever possible, it is wise to take advantage of opportunities.

Publications

As an aspiring new investigator, if you have no research or evaluation publications, we suggest that you collaborate with an investigator in your area of interest. These kinds of collaborations should lead to publications. This linkage usually begins with secondary authorship and progresses to primary authorship in a planned sequence of publications. The important outcome is that you will have publications describing your preferred methodology in your area of interest. If your application will include methods with which you have little or no experience, begin getting publications by working on projects with an investigator who uses these methods.

Research or Evaluation Review Function

Anything a new investigator can do to enhance research or evaluation reviewing skills is helpful. Reviewing research and serving on dissertation committees hones analytical skills, thereby furthering your ability to be precise and compelling in your own work. Take advantage of opportunities for reviewing research and evaluation papers, projects, and abstracts whenever they occur. Placing yourself in this position enables you to more effectively write your application with the review group in mind.

Collaboration and Consultation

Developing a research application is a collaborative effort. Rarely is it done alone. Keep in mind that the final production, including copying, collating, and mailing, is integral to success, and you must expand your resource network to include having personnel for these activities as well as your co-investigators from the outset. Collaborations build a network of relationships and information paths invaluable when developing a research or evaluation application.

Research or Evaluation Methods

Research or evaluation topics generally have preferred methods. Choose topics with methods that are within your range of experience and ability. The fact that the interpretation of findings is based on the result of the methods used, both design and statistical, should be motivation for remaining within your range of expertise or for choosing collaborators to expand available methods. However, even when collaborators have primary responsibility for certain methods, you should have the ability to participate in interpreting the results flowing from them.

Pilot Data

Pilot data are crucial to a competitive application and can be independently or collaboratively collected and analyzed.

Formal Courses

If you are interested in pursuing a research or evaluation topic that requires methods or analyses with which you are not familiar, take a course.

Research Hypotheses You Would Like to Test

If you are interested in testing hypotheses outside your area of interest or training, it might be best to be a co-investigator until you have a good grasp of the new area. For the most part, because of the extensive supporting material required, applications are most competitive when the hypotheses are within the realm of the PI's interest and experience.

Positioning

Infrastructure

Not all organizations have sufficient research infrastructure to qualify for financial support from external sources. If you are interested in doing research or evaluation and are employed by such an agency, one solution is to collaborate with someone at a research university. Another approach could be to seek funds to enhance your organization's capacity for funded research or evaluation projects. One example of such funding is an announcement from the National Institutes of Mental Health that describes the availability of funds to assist in the development of technical and scientific support for institutions with access to large and varied populations of individuals with mental disorders. A funded project of this type would serve as a solid foundation from which to request further funds for projects involving these populations.

Research universities generally have an infrastructure sufficient to support most kinds of research. It is critical that an investigator learn about the services and responsibilities of the various units. It is possible that the expertise you need is not only available but also freely given. This would be the case, for example, with a clinical research facility or a statistical unit that depends for its continued existence upon demonstrating its usefulness by providing a service for research or clinical projects.

Funding Source Identification

Research universities generally have a unit responsible for information dissemination on funding opportunities. If your organization does not have such a unit, you will need to develop a system for getting this kind of information. A most readily available source is the NIH Guide, which has information about funding from the National Institutes of Health. This publication is free upon request. The address for this publication, as well as other sources of funding information, such as the *Federal Register*, can be found in Chapter 7. Funding source identification is another area where linking can be beneficial. Letting people know you are interested in applying for research or evaluation funds usually increases your opportunities for learning about funding sources.

Colleagues

Because developing a project application is rarely an individual effort, networks of information and expertise must be established. If you have not established these networks, a place to begin is attending presentations, seminars, or classes in your area of interest. In our opinion, you must risk linking. That is, step up and make yourself visible to those with whom you might wish to collaborate. Do not wait for them to become aware of you. After making the first contact, follow up with a short note or telephone call.

Personal Characteristics

There are no quick fixes for problematic interpersonal relations, nor for the way each of us relates to our work. A strategy that can help is to develop and use structures that guide behavior in the appropriate manner. One technique, for example, that helps with assessing the level of excellence of previous work, the progress of current work, and the development of plans for future work is to use a work plan or timetable for the project application process (see Chapter 12). The advantage of a timetable is that it depersonalizes tasks, especially collaborative tasks, and provides a record of what must be done and when it must be done. Using a timetable relieves the PI of persuading co-investigators and other collaborators of the importance of the many tasks that must be done. A timetable lists the small tasks incorporated into every effort to develop a competitive application. When viewed in this context, the relevance of each task, however small, is obvious. It also provides a mechanism the PI can use to draw the attention of investigators away from the complete application—sometimes an overwhelming thought—and direct it toward selected parts.

Preview Your Role as a Funded PI

Read Chapter 15 of this book for a preview of some role expectations for funded investigators.

Begin!

"Whatever you can do, or dream you can, begin it. Boldness has genius, power, and magic in it."—Goethe

REFERENCE

Scheele, A. (1979). *Skills for success.* New York: Ballantine.

3

The Competitive Project Application

The competitive project application is a showcase for the principal investigator's expertise. In this chapter we explain how investigators can use the parts of the application to their advantage. It is our experience that a competitive application has an organization and style that serves as a backdrop to highlight the scientist's ability, the scientific importance and project relevance, the effectiveness of the research or evaluation design, and the elegance of data analyses. There is no magic or wizardry involved in achieving this showcasing. It is a product of activities, common to scientific pursuits, completed within a specified time. One of these activities, which is often not given sufficient attention, is taking time to think and plan, both alone and with others. The amount of time spent discussing planned research energizes a group's enthusiasm for the project. This enthusiasm can translate into sustained interest and often superior intellectual performance.

AUTHORS' NOTE: Part of this chapter is based on an article by Leukefeld, C. G., & Ries, J. B. (1993). Strategies to compete for federal grant funding for research on social work practice. *Research on Social Work Practice, 3*(2), 208-218.

The payoff for these efforts is an application that makes a persuasive first impression and a positive lasting impression at each of the application's reviews (e.g., peer review, staff or program review, and fiscal review).

The following comments are what a PI hopes to get from a review group, and exemplify the outcome the material in this chapter hopes to facilitate: "The writing style of this application is exceptionally lucid. Preliminary data have been clearly presented. In addition, well written and logically constructed arguments have been used to justify. . . . "

To that end, we present and discuss the primary components of the application. Their presentation forms the basis of a competitive application. In brief, a competitive application meets the criteria of the funding source, of good science, and of persuasive communication. The criteria specified by the funding source are usually straightforward. Good science is ordinarily a product of training, experience, and a focused research or evaluation plan with a theoretical underpinning. A persuasive application is a product of a researchable idea, thinking, careful writing, and consideration for the reviewers.

The funding sources vary in the extent of detail included in their description of the form and appearance of application components. However, an investigator must attend to what is provided whether it be sparse or voluminous. We suggest the following principle: Don't fight for control over the domain a funding source has claimed! However, maintain control of a vital aspect of the application: its quality. Quality, in a project application, is a function not only of the integrity and presentation of the research or evaluation plan, but also of the content and presentation of the entire application, which includes adherence to the instructions provided. Quantity is not as important as quality, and attention to detail is imperative.

An important step toward producing a quality application is determining the expectations guiding those who will review and judge your application. Research or evaluation grant application expectations arise primarily from two sources—the granting agency and the principal investigator. The decision to choose a particular funding source is essentially a decision to meet formal expectations related to content, timeframe, budget, and expectations concerned with the many details of the application materials. The funding source's research expectations are found in the charge given to application reviewers and those who make funding decisions. The National Institutes of Health (NIH) call these expectations review criteria. The PI also establishes expectations for the reviewers through the structure and content of the project plan. Your goal, as a PI, is to meet each of these expectations to the best of your ability, describing and labeling every aspect, procedure, and process.

No details are too insignificant for your attention. Keep in mind that many grant applications will be vying for funding from the same finite pool. It is important, therefore, to gain the competitive edge whenever possible. What this means is that a competitive application is written by an investigator who knows the basics, both the expected and the desired, and goes one step further by developing that unique combination of ideas, language, and structure that forces a "WOW!" from the reviewers.

An instance that highlights the importance of meeting expectations is the fate of an application submitted to an NIH institute in response to a request to examine the incidence and prevalence of a specific disorder. One of the authors and his colleagues proposed a study to examine the incidence and prevalence of alcohol and drug use in a specific group of U.S. health professionals. Although the review group stated that the proposal was sound, it received a promising but unfundable priority score because insufficient justification was provided for the study. The review group expected to see a clear and crisp justification for pursuit of the study, in terms of need and future use. They did not find it and could assign only a mid-level priority score. Reviewers needed to be persuaded that funding the research study would be a good investment of scarce resources. The need to defend the overall value of the project relative to its cost is easily overlooked even by seasoned investigators, simply because the project's value is self-evident only to the investigators.

To complete every detail according to instructions and the demands of science, over the course of a document that is as long as an application, is difficult and time consuming. The effort required to do this, however, is well-spent because the results are cumulative and inexorably lead reviewers to a clear understanding of the project and to a perception of overall excellence. A competitive grant application is the embodiment of new and exciting ideas presented in an orderly and comprehensible package. There is no getting around the notion of competition. Make no mistake: When you submit a project application for funding, you are competing for part of a finite pool of money, whatever the funding source, and no matter how many times you may have already been funded.

FUNDING SOURCE EXPECTATIONS

Mission Statements and Program Announcements

The funding source's priorities and expectations play a pervasive role and make excellent guidelines for the new investigator. A competitive application reflects the funding source's priorities. Reviewers expect an application to fall within the stated mission and established priorities. The following are some examples of mission statements.

- The Diabetes Research and Education Foundation established a priority "to provide seed grants to serve as catalysts for future programs in the treatment of patients with diabetes."
- A recent mission of the NIH was to improve the health of the citizens of the U.S.
- The Robert Wood Johnson Foundation has a mission statement to "make grants . . . to programs and projects designed to improve the health and health care of Americans."

An exceptionally well-written research plan with meticulous attention to scientific method and analysis of results submitted to any of these funding sources will not be funded if the topic is outside their mission. Most funding sources do not have a broad mission of funding good science or good projects, and many do not have a mission incorporating pilot, exploratory, or basic research with no foreseeable applicability.

An application submitted in response to a program announcement is expected to be congruent with that announcement. The following is an example of an announcement titled "Research on Mental Health Services in General Health Care" from the *NIH Guide for Grants and Contracts*:

> The goal of this Program Announcement is to encourage research on mental disorders in primary care and other general medical settings, particularly research that focuses on the nature, recognition, classification, treatment, and outcomes of people with mental disorders in these service settings. This announcement may encourage the development of needed research that seeks to improve understanding of how best to assess mental disorders and provide mental health services in general health care settings. . . . (U.S. Department of Health and Human Services, 1992, pp. 10-15)

An investigator whose project does not fall within the areas indicated in the announcement should not apply. It is that simple.

The principle we recommend you keep in mind during this phase of application preparation is: Choose the funding source carefully, adhere to the guidelines stated in the announcement, and pay particular attention to review criteria. Do not submit a grant application that is clearly outside the source's stated areas of interest, and do not volunteer your opinions to the funding source about the appropriateness of its priorities or interests. If you wish to express your opinions to a funding source, do so outside the application format.

Although you might identify a funding source that has a mission statement almost congruent with your interests, identifying a perfect match is difficult. If you cannot identify a funding source with interests precisely like yours, use your creativity to develop a project plan that enables you and a funding source to achieve desired outcomes. A principle that we believe important is that it is usually not a good idea to determine the interests of a funding source and then try to design that project. It is also not a good idea to try to develop one project that includes every interest of a funding source. Information on funding sources and their requirements are available in a variety of forms. We will discuss this topic in Chapter 4.

After identifying a funding source with interests compatible with yours and for which you believe you can meet both the topic expectations and the review criteria, additional funding source requirements need to be evaluated. These requirements are available in funding source publications and from the program staff. The following sample of funding source requirements are those we believe to be important because of their influence on the application preparation process and on the conduct and financing of a project.

Specific Requirements

A competitive application must reflect funding source requirements such as the following:

Application Deadlines

Deadline information is available from the organization and from its published materials. Choose an organization with deadlines you believe you can meet. In addition to application deadlines, some funding sources set deadlines for letters of intent or for receipt of preproposals or concept papers for review.

Eligibility

Some funding sources have preferences about the geographic region within which they fund projects (e.g., "Awards will be made only for research conducted in Kentucky"), while others are interested only in national concerns. Other kinds of funding preferences are for health or nonhealth related topics, individuals or institutions, PI credentials (i.e., faculty, postdoctoral or predoctoral), and the number of awards granted within particular topic areas.

Funding Restrictions

Funding arrangements need to be compatible with your project's requirements, your timetable, and the regulations of your financial affairs or business office. Some of the factors to consider include:

- Restriction of the funding period to a specified time (e.g., 2 years or no less than 5 years);
- Regulations about the amount of indirect (overhead) costs allowed;
- Maximum direct costs allowed and limitations on direct costs by year;
- Earliest possible funding start date;
- Option to extend research timeline with unexpended funds if required; and
- Option to carry over unexpended funds to the next research year.

Types of Projects

Funding sources have preferences for the types of projects they support. Some possible types are basic research projects, applied projects, evaluation projects, career development or training awards, curriculum development, and demonstration projects. Determine the type of project you wish to submit and apply only to sources that fund that type of project. In our experience, attempts to persuade a funding source to modify its funding policy by submitting a superior application most often fail to produce the desired results.

The application process is not the same for all types of projects. Although the application process is similar across and within funding sources from year-to-year, it can vary. Therefore, obtain a complete application package from each potential funding source and read it carefully. The material provided will possibly include information about the proposal format, forms required, applicant-organization approvals required (i.e., animal and human subject protection, institution drug-free status, and conflict of interest) and general guidelines, including information about the type size required, page restrictions, and document style. If information is not provided, you need to rely on your judgment and the opinions of colleagues for the best course of action. When information is critical to the research presentation, call the funding source and request more information.

Review Factors

Review criteria, procedures, and review group composition are not uniform across funding sources. Review criteria should be used to shape and outline the final application. A copy of the instructions the funding source sends to its reviewers will help determine whether weights are applied differentially to different parts of the proposal, whether your assumptions about the weight of each part are accurate, and whether there are review and other criteria you had not expected. We recommend, when possible, that review criteria be used as application headings to spotlight these important areas for the reviewers.

The composition of the review group is useful information. Review groups can consist of either university personnel or community members with a variety of backgrounds, or both. The tone and style of an application should address the particular configuration of the review group. It also never hurts to cite the work of review group members when appropriate. However, whatever the review group composition, it is best that a project plan, to the extent possible, be written in everyday language.

Application Instructions

A competitive application is completed according to all instructions provided. Each funding source has an application form designed to meet its information needs. An examination of application forms from a variety of funding sources reveals that some funding sources have fewer information needs than others. Some applications require many kinds of supporting documentation, whereas others have few. Some applications provide detailed instructions about how to present and sequence the project plan; others give none. We recommend that you not expect the instruction section to include all instructions. Check each page of the application for additional instructions and reminders. It is most important to follow all instructions so reviewers can find information in the customary places. Keep in mind that funding-source reviewers know the customary place for certain information to appear, and they expect it to be there! Follow directions carefully, especially directions about where and how the information is to be provided and the extensiveness requested. When allotted space permits only 250 single-spaced words, do not add a page, a line, or even a word!

It is critical that only the most current application form is used. If you have received an application packet from someone other than the funding source, make a telephone call to determine whether you have the most recent revision of the instructions. The NIH research grant application (PHS 398), for example, has this information on page 1 in the upper left-hand corner. If you have used a particular application package before, do not rely on your memory. Read the instructions again both to refresh your memory on the more obscure details and to assure yourself that your understanding of the instructions is correct. We also recommend that someone else read the instructions and check your final application against them.

Supporting Documents

The successful applicant will not only provide information in the expected place, but will also take the perspective that all the requested, and therefore expected, information contributes details used by reviewers to make approval decisions. Therefore, another principle to keep in mind is this: Do not view the application's supporting document pages as mere forms. They should not be passed along to someone else for completion, without your oversight. Regard each request for information as an opportunity to show your expertise, the ability of your organization to support your project, and the breadth of experience and knowledge found in your project group. It is less tiring to complete a competitive application if you can suspend judgment on the usefulness of completing any item as instructed. It does not matter whether it makes sense to you, or whether you find it inefficient, repetitive, or just plain useless. We have learned that if the instructions say "do it," then by all means make sure you do it.

Review Criteria

A competitive application embraces and incorporates the review criteria. Funding sources provide reviewers with general guidelines for judging the scientific value of project plans. Most project announcements include review criteria that will be used specifically for applications received in response to the announcement. The general criteria used to review the NIH individual research project applications are the following:

- Scientific, technical, or medical significance and originality of the proposed research;
- Appropriateness and adequacy of the experimental approach and methods to be used;
- Qualifications and experience of the PI and staff in the area of the proposed research;
- Reasonable availability of resources necessary to the proposed research; and
- Where an application involves activities that could have an adverse effect upon humans, animals, or the environment, the adequacy of the proposed means for protecting against such effects. (U.S. Department of Health and Human Services, Public Health Service, National Institutes of Health, 1992, pp. 13, 15)

An example of announcement-related review criteria are those included in the program announcement entitled "Research on Mental Health Services in General Health Care":

Applications will be reviewed for scientific and technical merit by the assigned review group in accordance with the standard NIH peer review procedures. Following scientific-technical review, the applications will receive a second-level review by the appropriate national advisory council.
   Review criteria include:

   Scientific, technical, or medical significance and originality of the proposed research;
   Appropriateness and adequacy of the experimental approach and methodology proposed to carry out the research;
   Qualifications and research experience of the PI and staff, particularly but not exclusively in the area of the proposed research;
   Availability of resources necessary to perform the research; and
   Appropriateness of the proposed budget and duration in relation to the proposed research. (U.S. Department of Health and Human Services, 1992, pp. 10-15)

Other examples of review group considerations are related to the administrative environment:

- Feasibility of the project within the resources and timeframes proposed; inclusion of specific written agreements with cooperating institutions
- Management capabilities, including fiscal administration, procurement, property and personnel management, planning, and budgeting

- Institutional commitment to new individuals responsible for conducting essential project functions

Given these kinds of general and specific review criteria, it is easy to see why applications funded by the NIH are characterized as:

- Presenting research that is significant and original science;
- Incorporating a methodology designed to test the proposed hypotheses or answer the proposed questions;
- Having a PI and other personnel with qualifications and experience sufficient to bring the project to a successful conclusion;
- Having available resources such as lab space, subjects, and statistical support for the conduct of the project;
- Budgeting both money and time in a realistic frame;
- Encompassing an area of study within the mission of the funding source; and
- Attending carefully to the details of completing the application according to the funding source's specifications.

THE RESEARCH OR EVALUATION PLAN

Writing the research or evaluation plan requires that you, as the PI, put into action everything that you know about preparing scientific documents. This experience may include writing journal articles, preparing reports about clinical findings, conducting a dissertation project, or preparing summaries of journal articles for classes. However, we repeat, reviewers of research or evaluation applications use different criteria than journal reviewers use. Not only the scientific excellence of the material, but also its scientific and empirical relevance are considered, and perhaps its cost-benefit ratio. It is critical that the application demonstrates expertise and knowledge in the scientific area and persuades reviewers that the research or evaluation is important and timely and that you, as the PI, are uniquely qualified to conduct it.

We believe that the following three characteristics are integral to a competitive research plan:

1. scientifically relevant research
2. scientific integrity
3. persuasiveness

Scientific Relevance

Thinking is the heart of science and, consequently, of the project plan. Competitive research or evaluation plans communicate the thought, logic, and creativity of the principal investigator. All aspects of design are included and presented in enough detail for the reviewer to comprehend the integrity of the scientific plan. Statistical analyses are appropriate and adequately described. Compelling discussions of the implications for future research and findings are presented. Successful completion of the project is ensured by providing complete information on the critical dimensions of procedure, size and scope of project, relevance, preliminary study findings, data analysis, and expected contributions.

The vehicle that conveys the PI's scientific talent is the entire project application. The project plan is often viewed as a reflection of the PI's work habits. Research or evaluation is an orderly and logical endeavor requiring attention to detail. It is expected that a research or evaluation plan exhibit the PI's competency in these matters. Research or evaluation plans have a consistent and satisfying internal rhythm when the reviewer's anticipation is fulfilled—that is, when a research or evaluation plan's structure and content clearly and efficiently meet all expectations set up by the principal investigator.

Integrity of the Scientific Plan

The PI sets up a series of expectations that begin when, and wherever, the reviewer reads the application. What this means is that a test of whether expectations are being met would be to read any section of the research or evaluation plan and determine whether the question to which it responds is apparent. For example, if a reviewer starts with the design and analysis section, she or he should be able to state the hypotheses; if the objective section is read first, the statistical design should be apparent, as should the content and boundaries of the literature review. It is useful for our purposes here, however, to consider the application in the order in which it is generally submitted, beginning with the title and ending with the conclusion. Key sections set expectations that, in competitive applications, are unrelentingly met.

Title

The title sets up expectations that once set are modified only at the cost of confusion. The title can contain information about the focus of investigation, the primary variables, and the applicability of the findings. For example, the title "Pregnant adolescents: Smoking and low birth weight babies" sets up expectations about the project's content. It is reasonable to assume from this title that the subjects will be pregnant adolescents, and that at least two of the variables will be smoking history and birth weight of the babies. Low birth weight implies a focus on negative health consequences of the baby but establishes no expectations for collecting data on the health of the mothers.

Objectives

The research objectives or specific aims of an application must follow through with the title's promises. Including material from other domains or areas of science precipitates the impression that the PI has not considered the problem sufficiently to get a tight focus. The title cited above does not indicate an intervention for pregnant teenagers. Thus an objective specifying a smoking cessation intervention using a nicorette patch would come as a complete surprise. The reviewers' expectations might now be shifted from epidemiology to an examination of an intervention, with consequent muddling of the remainder of the application from his or her point of view. Whichever might be the study's focus, the point is that the introduction of extraneous material promotes confusion because the focus of the project is now in question and consequent expectations cannot be met. Thus we recommend the following principle be followed: Do not randomly introduce material to demonstrate the breadth of your knowledge!

Literature Review

The literature review is focused on keeping the promises made in the objectives section. Cite the literature concerned with the objectives and discuss it in a balanced manner orchestrated to have the reviewers conclude that the next important piece of research in this area is exactly what you are proposing.

Design and Analysis

Expectations set in the objectives must be met in the design and analysis section without fail. Hypotheses must match the research or evaluation objectives. In addition to major hypotheses, minor hypotheses can also be tested. However, we strongly recommend that you not include hypotheses that are outside the scope defined in previous application sections.

Budget

The budget does not escape from previously set expectations. The personnel section must include an adequate number of personnel to conduct the research or evaluation as described. All personnel listed must be qualified to be a part of the project group. Requested equipment, supplies, and other materials have their beginnings in the design and analysis section of the project plan. Reviewers will notice if you neglect to include budget items to cover all project procedures.

Persuasiveness of the Scientific Plan

The application's total presentation contributes to its persuasiveness. The competitive application is crafted to provide the most complete and orderly presentation possible for the reviewers. Information is presented in a clear, concise, and orderly manner. Arguments are made in the proper order, and conclusions flow easily and naturally from clearly stated premises. The language is straightforward and technical terms are used only when absolutely necessary. The competitive application reflects the PI's excitement and confidence about the project. In effect, a competitive application leaves the reviewer defenseless against the seduction of eloquence.

In summary, a competitive application should consist of the following:

a. complete and carefully compiled supporting documentation, including investigator abilities and setting capabilities;
b. presentation of a carefully thought out and carefully written project plan that is scientifically relevant and within the purview of the funding source's interests; and
c. inclusion of key information such as a detailed procedure section, size of project, pilot or preliminary study data, and statistical analysis.

We will again stress the principle that the most important characteristic of a competitive application is that it fulfills the expectations set by the funding source. For example, the initial screening of a proposal by a funding source might include checking the number of pages, the sections, and the type size. If a proposal contains too many pages or if sections are missing, the rule that might be followed is "return to sender." End of application process!

Of equal importance is meeting the reviewers' expectations formed by information from the funding source. Funding sources communicate their guidelines in their mission statements, in the application information mailed to prospective grantees, and in the specific charge to reviewers about project characteristics of most interest to the funding source.

ACTION STRATEGIES

Reviewer Reaction

When your application meets expectations at a high level, reviewers are in a positive frame of mind. It is important that their response to your work is a positive up-and-down movement of their head, not a negative side-to-side movement. Therefore, as you write your application and deal with the inevitable frustrations, keep that head movement in mind. If you find side-to-side head movement or a puzzled expression when you or a colleague read the application, reviewers will also be moving their heads from side-to-side when they read it. Do not let this happen! Take the time to sort out the difficulties, and when necessary get help to reword sentences, restructure the design, or smooth transitions. The principle that we would like to stress is this: Great project ideas poorly presented and communicated can lose to well-presented and clearly communicated mediocre project ideas.

Choosing a Topic

To get started on preparing an application, begin with yourself and your interests, not with the interests of funding sources or colleagues. A second step is to review the interest areas of funding sources and search for a possible match. A third step is to examine your environment and collegial network to determine whether they can support the kind of project you are contemplating.

During these early stages, we recommend that you not limit your information search to the confines of a narrow project, but rather that you give your imagination free rein. It is our opinion that motivation and passion are more easily generated and sustained by prospects of completing the ideal project. Assume that your ability and that of potential collaborators to complete a project of superb quality are the only factors that dictate the content, procedures, design, and scope of the project. Of course, the final application might be more limited. The broad vision is likely to encompass several projects from which you can choose and provide information useful in preparing a competitive application, such as how the proposed project fits into a program of research.

Ask for Help

Ask for help whenever you are stopped by an informational barrier. The most successful investigator has not become successful by refusing help. Relevant and important information is often in the hands of others. Reach for it! Interestingly, the people we often envision as most difficult to approach are those whose jobs are to provide such help. For example, investigators often hesitate to telephone funding source program officers. Do not hesitate to call program officers when you have questions about a project. When you call, ask whether they have time to talk or to schedule a time for consultation. Take time with these discussions. Ask for impressions and guidance. These staff members generally know the research area well and will spend time talking with potential investigators who are cordial.

You might also want to spend time talking with colleagues and scientists who have received funding from the source to which you plan to submit. Keep in mind that most scientists are willing to talk about their projects and about the review process. Investigators are especially willing to discuss controversies or perceived difficulties they have had with a study section or review group.

Information Overload

Beware of information overload! Gather as much information as you can, but do not expect to understand and use it all. New investigators can be overwhelmed with information that experienced investigators assimilate easily. Accept these limitations without self-recrimination. It is better to use limited information to your advantage than to be paralyzed by too much information. A mentor can be most valuable in sorting through the information and designing specific strategies.

REFERENCES

Diabetes Research and Education Foundation. (n.d.). *Grant research application*. Bridgewater, NJ: Author.

The Robert Wood Johnson Foundation. (n.d.). *Guidelines for grant applications.* Princeton, NJ: Author.

U.S. Department of Health and Human Services. (1992). Research on mental health services in general health care, PA-92-103. *NIH guide for grants and contracts, 21*(32), 10-15.

U.S. Department of Health and Human Services, Public Health Service, National Institutes of Health. (1992, March). *Orientation handbook for members of scientific review groups* [Interim version], pp. 13, 15.

PART II

Key Connections

Opening Moves

4

Funding Mechanisms and the Review Process

This chapter focuses on funding mechanisms, and a sample of the special applications within them, through which a new investigator might obtain research funding. Information is also provided about the review process. Whatever the funding mechanism, awards, for the most part, are made to organizations such as universities or community agencies on behalf of investigators rather than directly to the principal investigator. Some foundations prefer to make awards directly to investigators, but these awards are the exception rather than the rule. A variety of grants are available from foundations (Dermer, 1980; Kurzig, 1981; Turner, 1986). Descriptions of funding mechanisms and special applications used by the U.S. Public Health Service are used in this chapter because of their detail and because other funding sources use similar descriptions. Deadlines vary with the funding mechanism, type of application, and funding source. Some applications are due once a year, others have only a specified deadline and no resubmissions, while others have three regular recurring deadlines each year. Each funding mechanism has a set of requirements peculiar to it. It is important that investigators be aware that the relationship between them and the funding source is different for each of the funding mechanisms.

"I've got the grant!" This is great news, but what exactly does it mean? It certainly means that a principal investigator's application has been funded. But was the award a grant or was it a contract? Noting the differences between grants and contracts is basic to a cogent discussion of governmental and foundation funding possibilities. To ascertain whether the award was a grant requires more information about the kind of research, the scope of the project, and the relationship between the PI and the funding source. This chapter informs new investigators of the variety of common research funding alternatives. The review process is different for grants and contracts. Chapter 10 presents a discussion of the influence review criteria have on the project development.

The issue of the kinds of research personnel required for a project arises early in the planning process and influences the choice of funding mechanism. Decisions made at this stage will have a significant impact on the composition of the project application. It is critical that the personnel, topic, and scope of the project mesh. In general, funding sources accommodate a variety of professional personnel to meet their needs and the needs of the investigator. We call these combinations "special applications." Although every funding source does not support a full range of special applications, those of both federal and nonfederal funding sources are often similar. Whether an investigator is located in an academic or community setting, it is prudent to know the characteristics of different funding mechanisms and special applications and to choose one that most closely fits the project requirements.

In our experience, we have learned that potential investigators, whether in an academic or community setting, do not always understand the differences in funding mechanisms. Three commonly used funding mechanisms are grants, cooperative agreements, and contracts. Funding mechanisms can be thought of as having two primary dimensions. One dimension represents the range of independence the PI has with respect to the project content (e.g., freedom to choose the method or approaches, the scope of the project, and data characteristics and use), and another one represents the range of collaboration and cooperation required to conduct the project according to funding source specifications. These two dimensions clearly influence the attractiveness of a funding opportunity and the competitiveness of an application. We have also come to recognize that many applicants, when they do not understand the distinction between a grant and a contract, have difficulties after receiving an award. We will first discuss grants, because the new investigator is most likely to use the grant funding mechanism and because most funded research, evaluation, and demonstration projects to academic and community settings are grants rather than contracts.

GRANTS

Research grants are financial awards in support of research projects with anticipated but not guaranteed outcomes. Grants permit investigators to design and conduct research from theoretical positions and with methodologies valued by the investigator. Grants, therefore, support investigators in their pursuit of scientific knowledge with limited restriction. The availability of funds is often publicized through announcements from the various funding sources.

Announcements describing the availability of funding for research grants can be divided into two broad areas: those in which the PI has maximum freedom about the research focus, methodology, and data collection (investigator-initiated grants); and those in which the funding source places some restrictions on the PI (funding source-initiated grants). Announcements also state the deadline for receipt of applications; some of these are recurring, whereas others are a onetime occurrence.

Investigator-Initiated Grants

Investigator-initiated research grants are usually submitted by individuals who want funding for a specific project. A grant application ordinarily arises from the desire of an investigator and his or her collaborators to pursue an interesting and important line of investigation, or to develop a specific program or intervention. Preferably the topic under investigation directs the scope of the project and the personnel requirements, which in turn affect the special application chosen.

Funding sources regularly publish announcements that specify current interests and descriptions of the preferred personnel configuration. The research applications most likely to be successful are those that follow the guidelines and address the areas of research targeted by the announcements. Research applications addressing other issues, however, are also accepted and reviewed if they fall within the mission of the funding source.

Popular special applications for investigator-initiated projects accommo-date a wide variety of research personnel configurations. They range from those with only a PI to those that incorporate an administrative core serving several large research projects or several pilot projects.

Sole Investigator (Collaborators Optional)

Examples of special applications for the investigator-initiated project with a basic personnel configuration are the traditional research grant, the new investigator award, and the small grant.

An example of a research announcement with this personnel configura-tion is one specifying a clinical area concerned with developing innovative clinical approaches for drug abuse treatment. The announcement, which might also describe the differential need for developing and examining psychosocial treatment approaches, might limit the therapeutic method only to those entailing interpersonal interactions, thereby excluding pharma-cological interventions. However, the research methodology, the scientific theory, or any other scientific issue would not be specified.

The wording of this kind of announcement suggests that an application with or without collaborators would be competitive and represents an opportunity for an investigator whose interests coincide with those outlined in the announcement. This example also shows how grants often combine restrictions and freedoms, permitting both the funding source and the PI to meet their objectives.

Depending upon the extent of his or her research experience and the size of the proposed project, a new investigator could appropriately choose one of the sole investigator funding mechanisms. A description of the funding mechanisms is included under the headings of Research Project Grant, First Independent Research Support and Transition (FIRST) Award, and Small Grant. Although the descriptions closely follow those of the U.S. Public Health Service, similar descriptions are used by nonfederal funding sources.

Research Project Grant. The investigator-initiated research project grant supports a discrete, specified project in an area representing the PI's interest and competency. The PI may be the sole investigator or may be assisted by or collaborate with other investigators. This is the traditional research grant, and the funding mechanism is assumed when a PI says, "I've got the grant!"

The key phrase for the new investigator in the above description is "may be assisted by or collaborate with other investigators." It is not uncommon for an investigator's research interests to require expertise in a discipline other than his or her own. Although the PI of a competitive application must have experience, publications, and preliminary data in the area of the proposed research, collaboration with other investigators can enrich the research and be a source of support. The collaborator who provides the broadest possible base for the new investigator is one with expertise, publications, and previous funding experience. Research projects are ordinarily funded for a maximum of 5 years; the minimum range is 1 to 3 years depending upon the funding source. The federal receipt dates occur three times a year and resubmissions are usually accepted.

FIRST Award. The First Independent Research Support and Transition (FIRST) Award provides research support for newly independent biomedical investigators to initiate their own research and demonstrate the merit of their own research ideas. These grants provide funding support for the first independent investigative efforts of an individual; provide a reasonable opportunity to demonstrate creativity, productivity, and further promise; and help in the transition to traditional types of research project grants. FIRST Awards, in most cases, provide funds for 5 years. During this period, newly independent investigators can establish their research programs and make significant and innovative contributions to their scientific disciplines.

The FIRST Award is designed for the new investigator who has an established research record but who has not been a PI on a major funded project. An investigator who has been a PI on a traditional research grant from the Public Health Service is not eligible for the FIRST Award. The advantage for the new investigator is that the review process takes into account the junior status of the principal investigator. The application instructions also make clear the availability of funding for mentors and consultants. This funding provides a broad base of support for a new investigator. The federal application receipt dates occur three times a year and resubmissions are usually accepted.

Small Grant. The small grant programs provide limited, relatively rapid financial support for research within the purview of a federal agency. Applications receiving priority are those meeting any of the following criteria:

- Less experienced investigators;
- Investigators at institutions with limited research resources and without a well-developed research tradition;

- More experienced investigators wishing to conduct exploratory studies that represent a significant change in the direction of their research; and
- More experienced investigators wishing to test new methods or techniques.

Review of small grant applications occurs at regular intervals, and resubmissions are accepted.

Multiple Investigators (Collaborators and Consultants Required)

The following are descriptions of some of the special applications that require collaborators and consultants. Although these descriptions follow those of the U.S. Public Health Service, which includes NIH grants, the opportunities for funding from nonfederal sources have similar descriptions.

Career Development Grants. Career development grants take a variety of forms. Some are for clinicians who are beginning a research career, others are for experienced researchers attempting to change the direction of their research, and still others are for the accomplished scientist who requires funding to support uninterrupted time to devote to a particular research project. This special application is very different from the previous three with respect to the extent to which collaboration and cooperation are required. The PI remains in control of the research; however, extensive collaborative and institutional support can be required. For example, a new investigator in an academic department may not only have to get approval for drastic changes in departmental responsibilities, but also might need to secure department commitment to the future support of his or her research-related activities. Federal career development grants have three regular receipt dates, and resubmissions are accepted.

Program Project Grants. Program project research is broadly based, multidisciplinary, and has a long-term, particular major objective. The program project is designed to support research in which funding several projects offers significant scientific advantages over support of these same projects individually. Successful program projects generally bring together scientists in diverse fields who might not otherwise collaborate. Thus an environment for multidisciplinary research is created, along with support of essential shared core facilities such as major equipment, laboratory test facilities, and research subject housing, perhaps in a clinical research center or residential facility.

Although a new investigator is not eligible to be a PI on a program project grant, he or she might be eligible to be the PI on one of the research projects within a program project grant. However, the PIs on the research projects are expected to be independent investigators. This special application provides an environment of support and cooperation that a new investigator with the proper credentials can use to his or her advantage. The program project grant does not represent an opportunity for a new investigator without publications in the specified area of research. In this sense it is more like the research project grant, and unlike the FIRST Award and the small grant, which require less research experience in the area of interest. Federal program project grants have three regular receipt dates per year, and resubmissions are usually accepted.

Investigator-Initiated Interactive Research Project Grants. The Investigator-Initiated Interactive Research Project Grants (IRPG) program encourages the coordinated submission of related research project grants (R01) and, to a limited extent, FIRST Award (R29) applications from investigators who wish to collaborate on research but do not need to share physical resources. These applications must share a common theme and must describe the objectives and scientific importance of the interchange of ideas, data, and materials among collaborating investigators. A minimum of two independent investigators with related research objectives are encouraged to submit concurrent, collaborative, cross-referenced individual research grants or FIRST Award applications. Applicants may be from one or several institutions. Applications will be reviewed independently for scientific merit. Applications judged to have significant and substantial merit will be considered for funding both as independent awards and in the context of the proposed IRPG collaboration.

This special application was announced in the *NIH Guide for Grants and Contracts* (Vol. 22, No. 16, April 23, 1993). By using it, a new investigator is as good a candidate for preparing a competing application as for the traditional research grant. There is an advantage in submitting an IRPG for areas of research that have expanded beyond single disciplinary boundaries: The IRPG provides an opportunity for complete research perspectives to be investigated, rather than attempting to include the necessary perspective in a single research project that could result in an application appearing unfocused. Federal IRPGs have three regular receipt dates per year, and resubmissions are usually accepted.

Instrumentation Grants. An instrumentation grant is an award for the purchase of major equipment for the improvement of an applicant's research environment. Instrumentation grants are important for research that requires expensive equipment not available to the PI because of deterioration, obsolescence, or restricted accessibility to available equipment. Instrumentation grants can be a particularly important funding opportunity for new investigators, who often bring new research directions to an academic department or community agency, and with that a need for new technology. This technological need most often cannot be met with a research grant because many funding sources are experiencing shrinking funds. For this reason, we recommend that funds for equipment be sought separately from the research application.

New and seasoned investigators must remain vigilant for instrumentation grant opportunities, particularly in research areas that are in a growth phase with the concomitant development of new designs and methodologies. These areas can require new or updated technological support, and on-site equipment can be particularly important for new investigators. Collaboration among new and senior investigators can strengthen an equipment application.

Funding Source-Initiated Research Projects

Another group of special applications focuses on funding source interests. These grant announcements are specific about the areas of research interest, and this detail is not to be ignored. To be competitive, applications must incorporate the interests of the funding source. The review criteria for the grants arise directly from these interests. It is common for the announcement to include the review criteria. The PI can use these criteria to assess the congruence of his or her plan with the requirements of the funding source.

Request for Application. The Request for Application (RFA) invites investigators to accomplish a specific purpose in a well-defined area of study by allowing them to choose their own method of achieving the stated research purpose. The receipt date is stated on the announcement; RFAs do not have recurring receipt dates. Letters of intent may or may not be required before submission. The lead time for RFA receipt dates is usually relatively short; it could be as brief as 8 weeks. Successful applicants are, therefore, investigators already involved in the defined area of study.

Although RFAs restrict the PI's area of research and the outcome measures, there is no restriction on the research design or data collection methods. There is also no specific requirement for collaboration, although collaboration is the rule rather than the exception. In our opinion, the RFA, because of the brief lead time, is not appropriate for a new investigator. The short lead time serves as a screening device for scientists already immersed in the particular area. This funding mechanism, however, does provide opportunities for new investigators to be co-PIs or co-investigators.

Center Grants. Center grants might be specialized center grants, comprehensive center grants, or center core grants. After funding, specialized centers provide shared facilities and resources to support multidisciplinary research in a specific interest area. The comprehensive center provides a basis for bringing together divergent but related facilities within a given community, such as a university with clinics, hospitals, and community agencies. Center core grants enhance an applicant's scientific environment and capability for conducting research, facilitating collaborative research, and supporting new faculty research. The avenues of research support for center grants vary. One avenue is an administrative core with financial support for small-scale pilot projects. In this case, the administrative core arranges for reviewing pilot projects and awards funds. Another avenue is an administrative core with research projects, in which the funding source reviews and awards the research project funds. The PI is advised to choose the avenue that best matches his or her research environment.

A center grant presents a package of restrictions for the PI. The funding source usually specifies a broad area or interest within which a particular center will specialize. However, neither the design, research methodology, nor, in most instances, the organizational arrangements of the shared facilities are specified. Center grants present opportunities for new investigators with expertise in the required interest area. Although new investigators would not be competitive as PIs, they could be project investigators on pilot projects or regular research projects. Especially helpful for new investigators are the projects that include small-scale pilot projects with the associated opportunities for research experience and publications.

Special Initiatives. An example of a special initiative is one that provides funds to underrepresented minorities in biomedical research. The National Institutes of Health (NIH) developed several programs that have been endorsed by each institute and awarding component of the NIH. These programs provide support for a continuum of potential investigators, from high school students to faculty members in institutions of higher education. These funds are available as supplements to PIs holding NIH research grants. The aim of these programs is to attract and encourage minority individuals to pursue biomedical research careers in areas within the missions of all the awarding NIH components by providing supplemental funds to ongoing research grants.

Research Supplements for Minority Investigators provide short- and long-term opportunities for minority investigators to participate in ongoing research projects while further developing their own independent research potential. The aim of these supplements is to attract and encourage minority researchers to focus their research on a targeted area of biomedical research. This is an excellent opportunity for qualified new investigators who need to build their resumes to be competitive as a PI on a project application.

COOPERATIVE AGREEMENTS

Federally employed scientists who work in collaboration with other scientists from nonfederal organizations carry out cooperative agreements research. This funding mechanism provides for direct involvement of the funding agency in the project design and also provides research support for portions of the project. Cooperative agreements, therefore, combine aspects of both the grant and the contract mechanisms, with the PI and the federal agency being partners in the project. A multisite research project of the National Institute on Drug Abuse (NIDA), for example, would require the cooperation of investigators from the coordinating center, collaborative treatment sites, and the NIDA Treatment Research Branch, Division of Clinical Research.

REVIEW PROCESS FOR GRANTS AND COOPERATIVE AGREEMENTS

A word is necessary at the outset about the length of time the review process takes. The following principle should be kept in mind: Do not let the process or the time the process usually takes wear you down. In the best of all worlds, an application for funds takes from 4 to 12 months to move through the review process. Although the review criteria, timeframe, and procedure for choosing reviewers are not identical for all funding mechanisms and special applications, the process an application moves through is similar, whatever the funding source. Given this, we will use the review process of the National Institutes of Health (NIH) agencies as our model.

The federal government and nonfederal funding sources are interested in providing systematic support for the strongest and best projects. To accomplish this objective, funding sources may use a one- or two-level peer review process. The NIH uses a two-level peer review process that begins with the assignment of an application to the study section or review group to which it is most closely related.

Study sections include from 16 to 20 scientists representing a wide range of specialties within a specific area. For example, a clinical and treatment study section in the drug abuse area might include psychologists, psychiatrists, behavioral pharmacologists, sociologists, epidemiologists, and special reviewers who have expert knowledge of clinical issues.

Each application is assigned to a primary and a secondary reviewer for an in-depth review and critique. During the study section meeting, these two reviewers present the application and discuss it with the other members. After the discussion, every member votes on the scientific merit of the application. Those applications that are judged to have scientific merit are then assigned a priority score by the members. The priority-score range is from 1.0, Most Worthy, to 5.0, Least Worthy. The study section's primary concern is with the scientific merit of the application, but the adequacy of the budget, in the context of the scientific goals, also receives careful attention. In addition to a priority score, the application is assigned a percentile rank, which indicates the percent of the section's applications that achieved an equal or better priority score. For example, a priority score of 1.55 and a percentile rank of 18% means that 18% of applications received a priority score equal to or better than 1.55.

After being assigned a priority score and a percentile rank, an application is sent to the Institutes' National Advisory Council, which concentrates on the application's importance for NIH's goals. The Council is made up of a panel of about 10 scientists and at least two volunteers from the nonscientific community who have an interest in the discipline associated with the applications under consideration. In addition to evaluating the application's relevance to the Institutes' programs and making recommendations for funding, the National Advisory Councils are also the policy-making bodies for each institute.

The Council reviews the grant applications and sends them to the specific NIH organization unit responsible for awarding funds. Funds are usually awarded according to the percentile ranks (lowest to highest) of the applications until the unit's funds are distributed. Results of the review process in the form of a written administrative summary ("pink sheet") are forwarded to the PI after the Council's review, about 9 months from the submission date.

Applicants should be aware that periodically changes are made in review procedures. For example, in early 1994 the NIH modified its procedures for evaluating grant applications (Ezzell, 1994). These changes, like many of those in the past, are often transparent to those submitting applications. The effect of modifications on application development is not apparent until after several review cycles. The changes in the procedures are motivated by an interest in effectively meeting the objective of funding the best scientific research designed by the best researchers. Participation in information and research networks is one way to keep abreast of modifications to review procedures and the effect they have on application development.

CONTRACTS

A contract is a funding mechanism used to secure a product or products according to a funding source's organizationally determined specifications. An example is the National Institute of Drug Abuse's solicitation for proposals to develop analytical methods, carry out quality control tests, prepare dosage forms, and perform stability studies for the compounds and dosage forms to be used in the Institute's medications development program. An investigator interested in doing this work requests the detailed specifications outlined in the Request for Proposal (RFP) package, decides whether he or she can do the prescribed work, and writes a competitive proposal.

The lead time for contracts is usually short. Proposal preparation time in the above example was 45 days. Contracts probably require more interaction with the funding source than any other type of funding mechanism. Unlike grants, contracts require regular and detailed progress reports. Some funding sources require annual reports, but most require more frequent reports. The funding source specifies the frequency and contents of these reports.

Contracts can be applied for from a variety of funding sources. However, we will use the federal procedure as our model because it includes many of the contract funding components and, therefore, is easily generalized to non-federal funding sources.

Contracts are advertised for bids. Contracts do not formally have PIs—the applicants are referred to as offerors or bidders. Offerors are expected to respond to the specifications described in the government's Scope of Work (SOW). Thus the applicant offers a written bid in response to the written parameters or specifications described in the SOW, which are listed in the *Commerce Business Daily, The Federal Register,* or the *NIH Guide.*

Most often, contract proposals permit little scientific or other creativity to be expressed. For example, a Public Health Service agency or NIH Institute might be interested in developing a study to examine the effectiveness of a clinical intervention in the United States. The potential applicant learns of the project through an advertisement in the *Commerce Business Daily.* Interested investigators telephone or write for the Request for Proposal package, which details the specifications of the project, from the governmental contracting officer.

The contract's SOW outlines the work plan to examine the effectiveness of a clinical intervention in the United States by describing the study parameters, including the number of subjects, the sampling frame, and the kinds of treatment to be included in the study along with other details. The SOW could also specify the sampling parameters, including gender, age, and race/ethnicity of subjects, as well as geographic location. The review criteria are also included.

The written bid or response to the SOW usually describes the methods and procedures, the type of staff, the timeframe, and the costs needed to meet the SOW's specifications and requirements. In other words, the contract proposal describes the approach that the offeror (a university, corporation, or community agency) will take to produce the specific product or services described by the government in the SOW. The intent of the contract bidding process, like a contract to build a building or airplane, is for the government to obtain the best product or service at the best possible cost within the specifications presented in the SOW.

An offeror may also be able to attend a bidders' conference, which is usually scheduled in the Washington, DC, area. A bidders' conference is a meeting where both governmental technical and program representatives as well as the contracting officer or a representative are available to provide clarification and answer questions regarding the announcement. This meeting is conducted in an open fashion so that an advantage is not given to one firm or organization. It is imperative that anyone seriously interested in submitting a contract proposal attend this bidders' meeting. However, the travel expenses, like the expense of preparing a contract application, are the responsibility of the offeror rather than the government agency.

CONTRACT REVIEW PROCESS

The contract proposals received by the government contract office within the specified deadline are reviewed in a closed meeting by a group of external reviewers. These external reviewers have no relationship with the offerors but are experts in the subject or product area. Rating criteria used to evaluate each separate proposal usually include staffing, plan for accomplishing objectives, and timeframe for delivering the product or service, but not costs. Reviewers score each proposal before attending the review meeting and discuss each proposal's strengths and weaknesses at the meeting. During this open discussion, reviewers may change their original score. Project costs are reviewed separately by the government contracting officer, not by the external reviewers.

After the review process, clarifying questions may be forwarded to those offerors who were within the competitive range and found to be acceptable to the external review group. Replies in response to specific technical questions are reviewed, and the external review group may be asked to rate each contract proposal again. Each proposal determined to be programmatically or scientifically acceptable is considered to be within the competitive range. It is then the responsibility of the contracting officer, in cooperation with the government technical staff, to make a final choice to award the contract, on the basis of the products or services proposed and the costs. Even after an announcement of a contract award is made, there is a possibility of an appeal by any of the offerors who did not receive the award. This could result in a lengthy process of examining the entire review and possibly in contract resolicitation and rebidding.

In summary, contracts are used to fund work within detailed specifications. This means that the offeror usually does not decide what is to be investigated, the methodology to be used, the data to be collected, or the final disposition of the data, but must be able to demonstrate his or her ability to perform the required work at a high level of accuracy and efficiency. Because a new investigator's research experience and publication record are limited, it is unlikely that a new investigator would be competitive in contract bidding. However, new investigators could appropriately be co-investigators on a contract and thereby gain research experience and enhance their research record.

ACTION STRATEGIES

Compare Research Requirements With Characteristics of the Funding Mechanisms or Special Applications to Make the Appropriate Choice

- Prepare an outline that includes the following:
    Personnel required and a description of their efforts during each project year;
    The extent to which you wish to control the project content, design, and methods; and
    Depth and breadth of your experience shown in your vitae.
- Review the funding mechanism characteristics presented in this chapter and select the mechanisms and special applications that can best serve your objectives.

Peruse an Extensive List of Funding Mechanisms

The Information Systems Branch of the Division of Research Grants of the National Institutes of Health publishes *IMPAC: A Computer-Based Information System of the Extramural Programs at NIH/PHS*. This publication, which can be ordered by calling (301) 402-0168, provides valuable insight into specific funds available from NIH.

If the research personnel and structure of your project deviate from the traditional one-site project with a PI, co-investigators, and consultants, consider funding mechanisms and special applications other than a traditional research project grant. Those described in this chapter, together with the extensive list provided in *IMPAC*, will help you to select the one suited to your particular project.

Note whether funding sources make awards to the PI or the applicant organization. If awards are made directly to the PI, contact your financial officer to determine your organization's policies in this circumstance.

Consider a First Independent Research and Transition Award

The success of new investigators attests to the feasibility of breaking into what has been called "the old boy funding network." FIRST Awards from the National Institutes of Health are designed to help new investigators receive funding. The provision of funding for mentors and consultants enables new investigators to write a competitive proposal, complete the research, and publish results in a timely manner.

Choose Collaborators

Collaborators can be an important asset to research and demonstration projects. For the new investigator, becoming a funded researcher usually requires early collaboration. It is important to identify and work with collaborators who find projects and studies exciting and can work with others in mutually satisfying arrangements. New investigators can have good results when they are able to identify able co-investigators and consultants who are enthusiastic about the project.

Contact the Funding Source

Most funding sources have program staff members who are the bridge between the investigator and the funding sources. It is important to talk with these staff members about your research. Think about what you want to do and the personnel and collaboration requirements you envision. Then call the program project official and ask when you might discuss your ideas. Sometimes a face-to-face contact will be suggested. If a face-to-face contact is feasible, then it is a good idea. But because of the time and money involved, telephone discussions are most common. When the call is made, be ready to take as much time as necessary to garner impressions and guidance about your application. The program project officials generally know the research area well and will spend time talking with cordial and interested investigators. The feedback you get about the structure of your project will be based on their knowledge of other projects similar to yours. Whatever structure you have decided upon, our advice is that you listen carefully to the suggestions so that you can think about incorporating them into your application when appropriate.

REFERENCES

Dermer, J. (1980). *Where America's large organizations make their grants.* New York: Public Service Materials Center.

Ezzell, C. (1994). Further changes ahead for NIH grant-review system. *The Journal of NIH Research, 6,* 35-36.

Kurzig, C. (1981). *Foundation fundamentals: A guide for grantseekers.* New York: Foundation Center.

National Institutes of Health. (1992). *IMPAC: A computer-based information system of the extramural programs at NIH/PHS.* Bethesda, MD: Information Systems Branch, Division of Research Grants.

Turner, R. (1986). *The grants register.* New York: St. Martin's.

5

Formal Resources

New investigators often do not know that they need formal organizational resources to complete a project application, nor do they realize the variety of formal resources available to them. Conversations with new investigators are regularly punctuated with questions such as, "Does anyone do that?" or, "Where do I go to get that done?" and statements such as, "I had no idea I would have to do that!" This chapter alerts new investigators to the formal resources that can be available and briefly describes the functions of these resources. Formal resources are usually easy to access because they are provided by organizational units whose functions are common knowledge. The personnel staffing these units regularly respond to questions, perform specific organizational services, and have knowledge of organizational functions outside their own realm of activities.

Identifying the organizational units that can facilitate the application process is critical to producing a competitive application. These units have the resources and the ability, and in some instances the responsibility, to address application requirements. Some services need to be requested, whereas others are an integral part of the application process and cannot be bypassed. For example, signatures of financial officers, deans, or directors are often required. With the trend toward collaborative and multisite projects, it is helpful for new investigators to be familiar with the formal resources at their own site and become familiar with those that exist in the other organizations within which they might find collaborators. This chapter discusses organizational units that can facilitate the application process. Because our focus is on the functions these units perform, we have elected to use generic labels, and we will present the units in order of their proximity to the new investigator. The department or work group is the first resource level; the college/university or the community agency is the second resource level; and the funding source is the third and final resource level. A chart of the three resource levels is presented in Table 5.1.

FIRST RESOURCE LEVEL

The first resource level provides services and resources only to its members. If this level is a university department, for example, the resources are available to that specific department's faculty but not to faculty from other departments. Ideally, unit members have access to or can compete for the level's resources.

Chair or Supervisor

The chair of an academic department, or a work group counterpart, can facilitate funding applications in a variety of ways, but the most important is by endorsing the effort. He or she can also direct a new investigator to a variety of organizational units that can provide information about potential collaborators and perhaps about a mentor. The first meeting arranged by a new investigator who has decided to apply for funding should be with her or his chair or supervisor. The new investigator should be prepared to discuss the proposed project and its impact on, at least, the following five resources.

Space

If research requires department or work group space currently in use or assigned on an appointment basis, the department chair must be involved in reallocation and rescheduling. Acquiring project space beyond that allotted can require the approval not only of the department chair or work group leader

Table 5.1 Table of Resource Levels

	Level 1	Level 2	Level 3
PI	*Chair or Supervisor* space time research funds pilot research funds approval	*Dean, Chancellor, Director* approval research funds	*Proposal Solicitations*
	Business Manager budget financial rules	*Office of Sponsored Projects* application forms research proposal structure final check before mailing mailing the application research interest list	*Program Descriptions* *Federal Programs* program project officer
	Research Coordinator application review	*Financial Officer* organizational regulations indirect costs contract negotiation approval	*Foundations* contact liaison
	Statistical Support statistician computer terminals statistical packages	*Budget Officer* prepare budget review budget	
	Manuscript Prep Assistance on-site printer photo copier word processing application review	*Institutional Review Board (IRB)* provide review forms approve human protocols	
		Animal Care and Use (IACUC) provide review forms approve animal protocols	
		Statistical and Computer Resources statistical consulting main frame statistical packages electronic highway information	
		Personnel Department rules and policies for hiring job descriptions pay ranges	

but also of a dean or other official. It is important to include the department chair, or work group leader, in these discussions so that your research space needs can be placed within the overall space needs of members at all levels.

Time

If a new investigator is located in a university and has a heavy time commitment to teaching and committee or service activities, or in a clinical department or a community agency with a heavy case load, research time priorities need to be set. Conducting research requires the new investigator's time in a variety of activities, many of which cannot be delegated. It is critical, therefore, that the new investigator and his or her supervisor agree to change the investigator's schedule or to discontinue activities so that the new investigator has adequate time to meet research or project obligations. Each situation is unique, but the outcome of discussions about the new investigator's time allocation must include sufficient research or project time.

Research Funds

Some funding sources limit the kinds of costs they will support. Some, for example, will not permit funds to be used for computers or equipment, whereas others will not allow funds to be used for investigator salaries. If a project is to be completed, anything in the project budget not supported by the funding source requires a second external funding source or support from some component of the new investigator's organization. Within the first resource level there is often incentive funding to help meet project requirements. If salaries are not supported by the funding source, the department or work group will often contribute. Again, each level-one situation is a little different; some units are able and willing to provide more financial support than others. The new investigator must know the limits of his or her level-one unit and apply for other funding to meet the project's needs.

Pilot Research Funds

A more compelling application is made when pilot data or pretest conclusions are presented. Complete or partial funding for these activities might be available at the first resource level.

Approval

Most organizations require that the new investigator's immediate supervisor approve the application before others in the organizational hierarchy. These policies can differ from one organization to another. It is important to know the official approval policy of all organizations involved in an application to avoid delays as the application mailing date draws near.

Business or Financial Manager

Business managers can be of great help in budget development. They have not only salary information but also the rules and regulations for fringe benefits, consultant reimbursement, travel expenditures, and indirect cost policies. They also often know the current cost of a variety of services and products. Because the new investigator's organization approves the proposed budget, the budget charges must be in line with all organizational policies.

Although budget figures are cost estimates, it is often difficult in succeeding years to secure funding in excess of that originally requested. Thus a business manager's knowledge of institutional financial trends can be invaluable when preparing a budget. This includes projected salary increases and the level of inflation for each budget category.

The budget is reviewed carefully by the funding source and becomes another opportunity for the PI to demonstrate competence. Professional assistance in preparing a budget insures that it will contribute to your positive image and that of the project. If the business manager at level one does not have experience with applications, the budget officer at resource level two might be consulted.

Research Coordinator

Research coordinators at level one can provide information about the unit's research efforts, interests, and resources. For example, a research coordinator in a university department can provide information about current research projects by others in the department, common interests among department members, copyediting, and appropriate statistical advice. In most cases this person can help a new investigator successfully negotiate some of the common pitfalls of application preparation.

Application Review

A research coordinator might also be able to do an item-by-item match of the table of contents and funding source guidelines, checking for omissions, deviations in format, incomplete information, or missing supporting materials. Not all deviations and omissions are equally serious. Reviewing instructions will determine those fatal flaws that must be changed before submission.

Statistical Support

Statistician

Having statistical support at resource level one is a distinct advantage. Academic departments often have a member who is skilled in statistical methods and research or evaluation designs common to the department's interests. This person can help assess the viability of a research idea, select a design, and evaluate data collection methods. In most situations, inclusion of a statistical consultant strengthens an application because of the statistical expertise needed during data collection and data analysis phases. Also, many reviewers, in the face of the fast pace of progress in data analysis and computer access to statistical programs, consider statistical consultants a necessity.

Computer Terminals and Statistical Packages

Computer terminals should be available to you for data entry and data analysis. If you plan to use a statistical package that is not already available on-site, find out whether it can be installed at your site and who will pay for it. If it is the only option for data analysis and no one in your organization can pay for it, then it must be requested in the budget of your application. If the preferred package is not available on-site and the cost is prohibitive, you should reconsider your design and data collection methods.

Word Processing Support

It is important that an assistant be available to do the word processing of the application. If you use a word processor, this assistant can generate the final drafts and produce the final copy of the complete application. If you do not habitually work at a word processor, this assistant must be available to provide immediate turnaround on completed application drafts. Clerical help must be planned for and not assumed. It is absolutely necessary to have access to timely and expert assistance during both the proposal preparation phase and the project implementation phase.

Some organizations have approved templates for the PHS 398 packet. If your organization is one of these, use the template in the preparation of applications requiring the PHS 398 packet.

Printing Support

When preparing an application, it is necessary to have an on-site printer and a photocopier to produce easily readable drafts and an excellent final original copy of the complete application. The variety of forms that need completion and the plethora of drafts produced before the final copy make this equipment essential. The Public Health Service has rigid type-size and line-size requirements; other funding sources might also have preferences. We suggest that you carefully read the instructions about the appearance of the final application so that the appropriate fonts are available when it is time to print the final application. Circulating draft copies to co-investigators is important. It is also important to create a good impression in all interactions with co-investigators, collaborators, and mentors. Circulating only clean, legible drafts is one means of creating a good impression.

On-Site Reviewer

An individual who is available to review the application before it goes into final production can be of great assistance. If you have a research coordinator, this might be one of the services offered on a regular basis.

SECOND RESOURCE LEVEL

The second resource level units provide services and approvals for several first-level units. Thus, their scope is broader, and access is usually less predictable, but important.

Deans, Chancellors, and Directors

Approval
The various levels of approval required by the funding source are specified in the application materials. In addition to these approvals, others might be

required by the applicant's organization. Within a university setting, the approval of deans, chancellors, and finance officers is often required before the application is mailed. These approvals are the official consent for the project to be done at the applicant's organization.

Research Funds

In some organizations level-two units may also have research funds that are competitively awarded. Although these funds are usually awarded periodically, there may be instances in which funds are given on an as-needed basis. These are funds that might be used for pilot research, equipment, large data analysis projects, or travel in instances where collaborators are from different geographical locations.

Office of Sponsored Projects

Offices of sponsored projects provide a wide range of services for project funding. Sponsored project staff can be enormously helpful in locating funding sources, securing application forms, and completing the application. Many research universities have well-developed offices of sponsored projects. Other research sites might provide these services on a limited scale combined with other administrative functions. The university offices of sponsored projects may also accommodate the research information needs of community agencies.

Offices of sponsored projects maintain current information about funding sources and their regulations. University offices subscribe to a wide range of publications that enable assessments of funding priorities for federal and nonfederal sources. In addition, some universities subscribe to the Sponsored Program/Project Information Network (SPIN), a computerized database of funding opportunities—federal, nonfederal and corporate—useful for identifying funding for research, education, and development projects. Information about funding is usually circulated on a regular basis to potential applicants. We suggest, if you have access to an office of sponsored projects, that your name and information about your research interests are known so that appropriate announcements and other information related to funding opportunities are forwarded to you.

Application Forms

Often a supply of application forms is kept in sponsored projects offices. If the office does not have a particular application, it can usually be secured very quickly.

Project Plan Guidelines

Sponsored project offices can also provide information about structuring a project application. The staff members in these offices generally have had experience with a wide variety of application formats and might be able to make suggestions when application instructions are not clear, or make telephone calls to clarify ambiguous application issues. In most cases the proposal structure guidelines are found in the funding source's application instructions. For example, the PHS 398 application provides detailed information about the structure required. However, some announcements require a nonstandard structure, and additional guidelines are sometimes ambiguous or not provided. Other publications on grant writing provide supplemental guidance (Coley & Scheinberg, 1990; Krathwohl, 1988; Lauffer, 1983; Ogden, 1991).

Final Check and Mailing

If applications are received in advance of the mailing deadline, staff members of sponsored project offices will usually review them for completeness. They will also review budgets for completeness and appropriateness. In our opinion, this is an important check, and an effort should be made to forward the application several days before the mailing deadline to provide time for review.

Research Interest List

The staff members of offices of sponsored projects at research universities most often compile lists of faculty and their research interests. This information can be helpful to the investigator planning a project for which a collaborator's expertise is needed. Collaborators are usually chosen from those with whom an investigator has previously worked. However, because this is not always possible, a listing of the research interests of others could provide names of potential collaborators. In many instances, those who maintain the research-interest list also know the names of those who have been funded and who publish regularly in a research area. A sponsored project office might also organize meetings for you and others interested in a specific project to explore interests and opportunities for collaboration. In addition to the usefulness of a research interest list in searching for collaborators, listing your interests can also be important.

Financial Officer

Financial officers know and implement financial regulations about allowable indirect (overhead) costs, contract negotiations for the organization, and approval of organizational commitments to funded projects, among others.

Budget Officer

A budget officer can help in developing budgets for all projects. A budget officer knows the rules and regulations of your organization, and often also knows the customary ways of presenting project application budgets. A budget officer can also assist in preparing a budget that is complete and comprehensible without intensive study.

Institutional Review Board—Human Subjects

Funding sources require that research projects involving human subjects be reviewed by an Institutional Review Board (IRB). The IRB reviews research applications involving human subjects in accordance with federal and institutional regulations. It is the responsibility of the investigator to seek IRB approval before initiating a project. The formal certification of IRB approval must be sent to the funding source. Certification requirements are not standardized and can range from a few items to an extensive form in the application, which must be completed by the investigator and signed by the institution's authorized official.

Funding sources vary with respect to the timing within which they will accept IRB certification notices. Some funding sources will not accept an application without IRB approval. Others will accept an application but must have IRB approval before review. For example, the National Institutes of Health will not review an application that does not have IRB certification before the study section convenes. Other funding sources do not require IRB certification until the application's funding status has been decided.

Under federal regulations, an investigator's application to conduct a research project involving human subjects can be processed by an IRB in one
of three ways:

1. exemption certification
2. expedited review
3. full review

The criteria that serve as a guide for a preliminary decision about which
type of review would be appropriate can be obtained from the human
subjects office. Any questions an investigator has about the conduct of
particular research and the IRB criteria should be discussed with the human
subjects office.

Some research areas might require respondent confidentiality and protection because of legal ramifications. This protection is granted by the Assistant Secretary of Health. The authority in PL 100-607 states:

> The Secretary may authorize persons engaged in biomedical behavioral, clini-
> cal, or other research (including research on mental health, including research
> on the use and effect of alcohol and other psychoactive drugs) to protect the
> privacy of individuals who are the subject of such research by withholding
> from all persons not connected with the conduct of such research the names
> or other identifying characteristics of such individuals. Persons so authorized
> to protect the privacy of such individuals may not be compelled in any Federal,
> State, or local civil, criminal, administrative, legislative, or other proceedings
> to identify such individuals (Public Health Service Act, Section 301(d), 42
> U.S.C. Section 241(d), as added by Public Law No. 100-607, Section 163,
> November 4, 1988).

A confidentiality certificate must be requested by the PI when research
requires respondent protection. Reviewing IRB criteria and discussions with
IRB staff can be most helpful. This is particularly the case for methods that
are physically invasive and those that require respondents to reveal sensitive
information.

Given the variability of funding source requirements with respect to
submission of IRB certification, it is important to understand IRB procedures for receiving and reviewing protocols. It should be noted that this
information will influence the sequencing of application preparation and
enable you to meet the funding source requirements.

Institutional Animal Care and Use Committee—Animal Subjects

Funding sources require that research using animals as subjects be reviewed by an Institutional Animal Care and Use Committee (IACUC). This committee has the responsibility for assuring the appropriate care and treatment of all laboratory animals used in teaching and research activities. The IACUC has the authority to review, approve, require research protocol modifications (to secure approval), and withhold approval of protocols involving laboratory animals. Because the IACUC is bound by federal and university (local) regulations, procedures vary from one location to another. It is important that new investigators who plan to use animal subjects contact their Institutional Animal Care and Use Committee for complete regulations and requirements for obtaining approval.

Statistical Consulting, Data Management Services, and Computer Resources

Statistical support services are staffed by statisticians who are available for consultation and for analyzing data. The configuration of these units is not standard, but it can be assumed that unit staff can work with you or can direct you to appropriate resources.

Data management services, when available, are valuable and should be used to the greatest possible extent. The range of services offered will vary from one organization to the next. The most comprehensive level of service would be accepting data over telephone lines and handling all aspects of it while remaining in consultation with the investigator until the project is concluded. The manner in which data are handled is an important issue to reviewers; therefore, it is advisable to seek out all of the data management resources available to you.

Computer resources include instructions for statistical packages and other computer software, and provision and maintenance of major computer hardware, rather than for research design and statistical analyses. We strongly suggest that before you make a final decision about a particular statistical analysis, you check the availability of computer software within your own organization. The quantity and variety of available computer programs have grown tremendously, and most often no single computer installation supports all available programs or the current versions, but rather has a limited configuration.

Personnel Department

Some project personnel, such as research assistants or data entry technicians, are usually hired through the personnel department. Before getting involved with budgeting for these positions, we recommend you consult the personnel department for a range of the salaries and fringe benefits for those positions included in the application. It may not be possible to outline precise job descriptions, but you will be able to determine broad categories for the positions so that you can make reasonable budget estimates. You will also need to know organizational policies about advertising the positions you wish to fill, and about the procedures for advertising, interviewing, and hiring.

THIRD RESOURCE LEVEL

The third resource level is the funding source. Once you have decided to apply for funding, it is necessary to communicate with a representative at this resource level.

Proposal Solicitation and Program Descriptions

Proposal solicitations and program descriptions advertise the interests of funding sources and provide sufficient information to potential investigators to establish interests. Funding sources distribute proposal solicitations that contain information ranging from detailed descriptions of desired projects to global descriptions of funding source interests.

Federal Programs

Federal agencies distribute solicitations for proposals on a regular basis through several publications, including the following:

The *NIH Guide* is published several times each month. This publication presents program announcements, Requests for Applications (RFA), and Requests for Proposals (RFP) or contracts. Each announcement includes a detailed project description, review criteria, budget limitations when applicable, and the names, addresses, and telephone numbers of contact officers. A personal subscription can be obtained free of charge from the NIH Printing & Reproduction Branch, or copies of the guide might be available through your organizational unit that provides support for research applications.

The *Federal Register* is another source readily available either through personal subscription or from an application support unit. The *Federal Register* provides detailed descriptions of all federal rules, regulations, and funding. It is very detailed and usually only selected parts are important to project investigators.

Healthy People 2000: National Health Promotion and Disease Prevention Objectives outlines the major chronic illnesses, injuries, and infectious diseases of interest to the Public Health Service, and is a statement of national priorities and opportunities. It is available upon request from the U.S. Government Printing Office.

Foundations

Organizations such as the Robert Wood Johnson Foundation, the American Cancer Society, and the Ford Foundation publish and distribute announcements concerning their interests to those on their mailing list. This information is also available from foundations upon request, or from your organizational unit that provides project application support. However, not all foundations regularly mail materials to prospective investigators. If you are interested in submitting an application to a particular foundation, request information about its mission and the types of research it funds.

Funding Source Contact Person

Your organization's funding source contact person can provide information about priorities and can assist investigators in matching their objectives and research design preference with the funding source's mission.

Federal Programs

The bridge between the investigator and a funding source for federal programs is the program project officer. Program project officers, who are usually professional scientists familiar with cutting edge research, are interested in receiving good proposals because their agency's existence and funding level are governed by the quality of funded projects. Program project officers look for projects that can win national and international recognition, expand knowledge, and be a forerunner for the development of needed and useful information or products. The program project officer is, therefore, an important person to contact about project ideas, methods, and objectives and also to recruit as an advocate.

The program project officer can provide feedback about the following:

- the appropriateness of your project area for a specific agency;
- the funding mechanism;
- the project design;
- the kinds of personnel that would be appropriate given your status, location, and the funding mechanism selected; and
- both the allowable budget items and the bottom line.

Program project officers can be most helpful when your project is focused and you have written a clear statement of project objectives and methods. Sometimes, if the program project officer considers it useful, she or he will volunteer to critique a concept paper or preproposal. This is a valuable service and should be used.

Foundations

Foundations and other private funding sources may or may not have a contact person. Larger funding sources such as the Robert Wood Johnson Foundation, the Carnegie Corporation of New York, the Ford Foundation, and the American Cancer Society have contact liaisons who play the role of a program project officer. Some foundations, however, do not have individuals who fill this role, but they do provide general and limited information over the telephone. In this case, gather as much information as you can about the following:

- the appropriateness of your idea for foundation funding;
- its customary level of funding;
- the application process—that is, whether a complete proposal is preferred or whether, as an initial step, a letter describing your interests is preferred; and
- the appropriateness of scheduling a face-to-face meeting to discuss your project ideas.

ACTION STRATEGIES

Determine the Kinds of Formal Resource Structures Available to You

Organizational information is generally available from a department chairperson or supervisor. This information can serve as a starting point for determining the scope of available organizational resources. As you identify organizational resources, we suggest you visit the office and collect the descriptive material about their services. Note carefully those services that you can or cannot use and those that are mandatory.

Assess the Usefulness of the Available Services

Discussing the usefulness of support services with those who have submitted applications for funding can be important. Sometimes a service is not as useful as one would believe, or the service can be found in a more accessible location. We have found that some services get very high ratings and have a reputation for helping to speed investigators on their way to completing applications.

Be Courteous

All of the encounters you have with people at the different organizational levels should be pleasant. The chances of this are better, we believe, if you are courteous and adhere to professional standards of conduct and attire in all interactions with organizational personnel. Issues related to interactions and relationships are discussed in Chapter 9.

REFERENCES

Coley, S. M., & Scheinberg, C. A. (1990). *Proposal writing.* Newbury Park, CA: Sage.
Krathwohl, D. R. (1988). *How to prepare a research proposal: Guidelines for funding and dissertations in the social and behavioral sciences* (3rd ed.). New York: Syracuse University Press.
Lauffer, A. (1983). *Grantsmanship* (2nd ed.). Beverly Hills, CA: Sage.
Ogden, T. E. (1991). *Research proposals: A guide to success.* New York: Raven.
Public Health Service Act. (1988). 301(d), 42 U.S.C., 241(d).
U.S. Department of Health and Human Services, Public Health Service. (1990). *Healthy people 2000: National health promotion and disease prevention objectives.* Washington, DC: U.S. Government Printing Office.

6

Informal Resources

This chapter focuses on the availability of informal resources. Informal project application resources are designed for a variety of purposes but are useful to anyone developing an application. We believe that investigating informal resources will be profitable. Keep in mind that first impressions are quickly made and difficult to erase.

We think of informal resources in two categories: a) those that are useful without anyone knowing your aspirations to be an investigator and b) those that require you to declare yourself as an investigator. When beginning, you might not want to become visible to your colleagues as a potential investigator until you have a fairly solid project plan, or until you feel comfortable within a research network. This approach is more fully discussed in Chapter 9, "Relationships and Interactions."

Informal resources are used as an information source by seasoned investigators and can also provide information to new investigators. Discussions with funded investigators can be especially helpful. For example, a new investigator can learn about project development by asking questions and by listening to volunteered discussions, particularly those about various obstacles. Formal and casual discussions can be windows into research or evaluation interests and into the work and interaction styles of potential collaborators. As you may have observed, some of us have a primary work style of dashing to meet last-minute deadlines, whereas others plan and complete work in advance. Interaction styles also may vary from those that are abrupt and terse, sometimes bordering on rude, to those that are expansive and detailed, sometimes bordering on boring. Knowledge of these approaches can direct your behavior and improve the first impressions you leave.

When it is suggested that a new investigator work with a collaborator in another area of expertise, we suggest that the new investigator learn whatever he or she can about that area. National meetings and 1-hour seminars concerned with the collaborator's research interest can be gateways to improved knowledge and new acquaintances. The discussions can provide information about the kind of research preferred and the type of data analyzed. It is possible that a new investigator could learn an approach that she or he has been considering is not feasible. Again, much can be learned before you declare yourself a potential principal investigator. The time to let others know your plans is after you have a fairly good grasp of what you expect from a collaborator. Careful investigation of the project area enables you to make a good presentation and create a positive impression when the time comes to recruit collaborators and consultants. Developing a reputation as someone who plans to submit an application but never does is to be avoided.

Whether you are positioned in a university or in a community setting, informal resources are available to you. Informal resources are important because they provide network entry. Some investigators prefer to work alone (either because it is their preferred work style or because competition in their topic area is keen) with minimal collaboration or contact with others, whether these people are administrative staff or other researchers. It is difficult, in our opinion, to submit a competitive application without collaborators and support services. An individual working alone is less likely to be aware of rumors and gossip that could be useful and of the barriers to application completion that seemingly appear out of nowhere.

CHANCE MEETINGS

A resource often overlooked is chance meetings with colleagues. Hallways can be especially productive places. These chance meetings provide opportunities to become involved as part of a group discussion or to initiate conversations. Sharing a common research topic is not always a requirement for a useful conversation to evolve. Hassles with computers and administrative personnel, as well as dilemmas about data coding, data collection, and statistical techniques, are common research-related topics. It is also common to hear, "Do you know where I can find. . . . ?" Usually, because of the overlapping issues in the research community, these conversations can provide at least one piece of useful information. If you have a question or dilemma, these conversations might be an appropriate place to raise it.

SCHEDULED MEETINGS

Information presented at scheduled meetings about research, statistics, and other general information can be put to good use in a research application. Because these meetings are not directed at those planning to be investigators, you can maintain anonymity.

Classes

When basic information is needed, classes are most helpful.

Regular University or College Courses

College or university classes that require a semester or quarter of attendance provide the most benefit but require a large investment of time.

Short Courses

Universities and colleges offer a variety of short courses that might meet for a period as short as 1 to 2 weeks or as long as 8 weeks. Investigate the availability of such courses by calling a registrar, a department chairperson, a computing center, or an evening course director. Short courses are also offered through community programs sponsored by city governments. Information about course schedules and the range of subject matter covered can easily be obtained. If you can find no specific source of information, call a library.

Workshops

Workshops are offered across the country on a variety of topics. Workshops last from one to several days. Information about workshops is probably already in your "junk mail." If you are not getting notices about an area of interest, talk to one of your colleagues about the offerings she or he is receiving. Examples of the kinds of workshops that can be useful to a new investigator are those on statistics, use of computers and computer statistical packages, management techniques, interpersonal relations (e.g., how to work with difficult people), communication skills, and organizational skills. When you get positive responses to your inquiries, request to be placed on mailing lists so you can use each of the resources to its greatest advantage.

1-Hour or Lunchtime Seminars

Lunchtime or 1-hour seminars are regularly scheduled in the academic environment and also in community agencies. These seminars attract information seekers and, perhaps more importantly, people with similar research interests. These sessions can provide opportunities to meet new people and catch up with current and former colleagues. The critical characteristic of these seminars is the tight focus of the material and the discussions. Problems in research concepts, designs, and related data analysis are fair game. Seminars also provide a convenient atmosphere for making initial contacts with potential colleagues; these contacts can be followed with a phone call or further discussions.

New investigators in the early stages of project planning who may not be ready to publicize their intentions to submit an application can use the 1-hour seminar to their advantage for obtaining opinions about research—particularly funded research.

Information about seminars is available from university department offices and agency directors. Wherever you are located, request to be placed on the mailing lists of university departments that host seminars in your areas of interest. Once you begin attending seminars, you become part of an information network.

National Meetings and Publications

National meetings provide opportunities to obtain an overview of current discipline interests and research areas, learn about preferred research designs and data analysis techniques, and meet and work with potential collaborators and consultants. It is important to have a sense of what is going on at the national level in your area of research or evaluation because your project will compete at this level.

Funding Source Sessions

Funding sources often send representatives to national meetings. Their discussions and conversations with other PIs can be helpful in assessing the research trends, with respect to both content and methodology.

Publications

Some professions and disciplines also collect and publish information about the availability of research funds. For example, information about funding available to nurses appears in publications such as *Nursing Research, American Journal of Nursing, Council of Nurse Researchers Newsletter,* and *Nursing and Health Care.*

Colleague Review

An individual who is available to review your draft application before it goes into final production can be of great assistance. This might be someone who has been funded, a research coordinator, or a colleague familiar with the application issues.

Final Internal Checks and Reviews

Before submitting a proposal, examine it from different perspectives. Locate a colleague who has received reviewers' comments from submitted research. These comments, even for projects not exactly like yours, highlight basic characteristics of a fundable application. Looking at such comments will provide insight into what reviewers address overall and into the specific features about which they express positive and negative comments.

We also recommend that an application be reviewed for content and logic by at least one individual who has not participated in its preparation. As stated previously, not all deviations and omissions are equally serious, but incomplete information in a procedure section, faulty logic, or a weak study rationale seriously impairs the competitive potential of an application. Someone who has not been a part of the production will read and reason with a fresh perspective to spot problems with procedures, statistical analysis, and logic. In addition, having a colleague do an item-by-item match of the table of contents or the funding source guidelines against the application will uncover omissions, format deviations, and incomplete information in the research plan or the supporting materials.

INFORMAL ORGANIZATIONAL SUPPORT FOR
CONDUCT OF THE PROJECT

Pilot Research Costs

In some cases, the new investigator will believe that an application will be more competitive if pilot data are available or if costs of pretesting new instruments are not included. Sometimes, although not broadly advertised, resources for these kinds of research are available in departments, colleges, or agencies if an individual can make a persuasive case for the need and the ultimate benefit of the expenditure.

Printed and Electronic Material

Books are available about every aspect of a project application. Some books focus on research design, statistical analysis, theories, research findings, and instrumentation. Other books are also concerned with improving organizational skills, writing skills, communication skills, and motivational skills. Although the latter are not resources investigators gravitate to initially, it is wise to assess one's personal abilities in these and other related areas to shore up competence and confidence.

Electronic material is also available. Software packages for statistical analysis and the electronic discussions available through LISTSERV provide a bird's-eye view of the kinds of problems investigators have with design, data, and data analysis. A broad range of information and research papers are also available through the Internet system. It is our recommendation that investigators develop competence in accessing both print and electronic material. These information sources can facilitate engagement in the professional networks of investigators.

ACTION STRATEGIES

Review Your Daily Schedule

Before you can take advantage of informal resources, you need to make a commitment to expand your information and your contacts within the research community. Reconsider your schedule from this point of view and try to free up time so you can participate in lunch-hour seminars, national meetings, and the occasional coffee break with a potential colleague.

Collect Information on Classes, Seminars, Workshops, and National Meetings

You probably will not choose the most useful event at the outset, but after attending several lunchtime seminars and a short course or two, you should be able to make educated decisions about the usefulness of advertised activities. Attending also enables you to broaden your network. It is possible that the seminar you choose might not be what you expect, but you might learn about others that are more in keeping with your interests.

Talk With Others

One of the things we have learned over the years is the necessity of developing and maintaining informal telephone and personal contacts with others interested in the same research or project area. In our experience, conversations of this kind are both more fruitful and more enjoyable when both parties give and take information. Remember the issues colleagues are interested in and volunteer what you have discovered since your last encounter. Asking questions such as, "So what is your latest project?" or, "How is your . . . going?" or, "Remember our conversation about . . . ? Well, I have learned that. . . . " are most promising entrees into learning more about ongoing research. Being a part of the investigator-information exchange system is a key way to strengthen your place in a research network.

The Administrative Maze

Many individuals feel overwhelmed when faced with a myriad of administrative details. Although the way these situations are handled need not be indicative of our ability to effectively handle research details, reviewers might use the lack of attention in these areas as an indicator of research ability. If you feel overwhelmed in matters of administrative detail, open conversations with those who have apparently conquered the beast. Often, a solution is to develop strategies that can then be used without fail because they result in a finished, quality product. Checklists or timetables can be used. Perhaps a friend can be used as a manager during application development. In the process of explaining requirements, you might come to a new understanding of the process and consider handling it on your own. The point that must be emphasized here is that you are not delegating responsibility when you use this kind of assistance: It is still your responsibility to provide complete, accurate, and timely information in the application. Reflect on your past success in organizing material and its flow through time. If you rate yourself low, do not hesitate to seek assistance. Denying the need can very well be detrimental to the final review of your research application.

Use the Electronic Highway

If you have access to Bitnet or Internet e-mail you can participate in LISTSERV lists. SAS-L, STAT-L, SPSSX-L, and VALIDATA are some of those available. If you want to determine if there is a list for a particular topic, send the e-mail message *list global/keyword* to your nearest LISTSERV or to LISTSERV@UKCC.UKY.EDU. Neither a name nor a subject need to be entered in the message. For example, if you were interested in a discussion list about epidemiology the message would be *list global/epidem*. You would then receive all discussion lists that begin with *e p i d e m* in their name. Using only a set of the initial characters returns all lists that have names beginning with those characters, thus providing a broader inclusion.

7

Funding Sources

Criteria for selecting a funding source often become obvious after you outline your project and know the restrictions under which you will conduct it. In this chapter we describe the most common types of funding sources. We also provide a checklist of funding source restrictions that might influence an investigator's decision.

CHARACTERISTICS OF FUNDING SOURCES

In the broadest terms, funding for research, education, and development projects is available from federal and nonfederal sources. The similarities and differences among the funding sources that support research, evaluation, and community demonstration projects are important considerations when choosing a funding target for an application. A major principle to keep in mind is that developing a competitive application begins with a scientifically viable question or hypothesis, not with funding limits, requirements, and a funding source mission statement. A corollary to this principle is to let the focus and type of the project direct your funding source search.

Federal Sources

Federal funds are awarded on the basis of applications or bids submitted by institutions on behalf of individuals who wish to conduct the project. Unsolicited applications are accepted, but most often applications and bids are submitted in response to program announcements, Requests for Applications (RFA), or contract announcements called Requests for Proposals (RFP).

A popular perception that federal funding is ubiquitous should not lead to the erroneous conclusion that it is not directed. On the contrary, a defined structure is responsible for the distribution of awards to support research, evaluation, education, and developmental projects. Congress makes the broadest award decisions through budgets they authorize to agencies that make the project awards. These funds must be awarded during the fiscal year of the appropriation, and future appropriations are contingent upon the success of funded projects. Each agency directs its funding to specific areas of interest. The interest areas of the agencies are delineated in their mission statement, published announcements, or listings of previously funded projects. The Department of Health and Human Services will be used as an example of how funding is directed.

Some of the units for which the Department of Health and Human Services receives funding are the Public Health Service (PHS), the Office of Human Development Services, the Social Security Administration, and the Health Care Financing Administration. These agencies disburse the funds to the offices within their purview. For example, the Public Health Service appropriates funds to operating agencies such as the National Institutes of Health, Substance Abuse and Mental Health Services Administration, Centers for Disease Control and Prevention, and the Food and Drug Administration.

In our opinion, the more familiar a new investigator is with the federal system, the less intimidated he or she is by the application process. However, competitive applications can be submitted without an understanding of the entire system. Each agency and institute clearly states the areas of interest in its publications and provides, upon request, complete application materials with instructions.

Although federal agencies have many similar procedures, there are also differences. An important difference is that not all the funding mechanisms and special applications discussed in Chapter 4 are used in all agencies or program areas. Sometimes announcements provide information on the funding mechanisms that are appropriate. If this information is not given, or if you are submitting an unsolicited application, which we do not recommend, check the agency's promotional material and call the agency to determine which mechanisms and special applications could be used.

Funding Interests

The funding preferences of various federal agencies are available from a variety of publications. An annual publication of sources of federal agency funding is the *Federal Funding Guide*. As previously noted, the *Federal Register*, a daily publication, publishes the current federal grant opportunities. Another federal publication, the *Commerce Business Daily,* describes federal contracts which are being put out for bid. Information for ordering these publications can be obtained from the Superintendent of Documents, U.S. Government Printing Office, Washington, DC 20402; phone number (202)275-2981. The NIH publicizes its interests in the *NIH Guide*, a free publication available by mail. Other information sources are listed under "Action Strategies" at the end of this chapter.

The following is a list of some of the federal agencies interested in behavioral, biobehavioral, and educational projects:

Department of Agriculture
Department of Commerce
Department of Defense
Department of Education
Department of Health and Human Services
Department of Justice

Review Procedures

In Chapter 4 we described the peer review system at NIH to provide a baseline for understanding other review procedures. The peer review system is common across federal agencies, although the structure within which it is implemented can vary. The peer review system is implemented by scientists who are familiar with the research area. Reviewers focus not only on technical aspects and methodology but also on the relevance of the project to scientific theory or potential application. The investigators' qualifications, the adequacy of research facilities, and the likelihood that the research can be carried out successfully in the time proposed are also taken into consideration. However, after peer review and review by the council, the final funding decision, based upon priority score and percentile rank, legally rests with the director of the agency. Because peer review is an advisory process, it is necessary to get a good review, but a good review is not sufficient for getting funded. It is, therefore, important to know as much as you can about the review process and about the funding source's priorities because of their influence on the design of your application.

National Science Foundation

The National Science Foundation (NSF) is federal agency that supports basic and applied research in most scientific disciplines. Clinical research is not supported by the NSF. Research on the etiology, diagnosis, or treatment of physical or mental disease, abnormality, or malfunction in humans or animal models of these conditions is also not funded. The most common award is the traditional research grant.

Nonfederal Sources

Nonfederal sources of project funds span a wide variety of organizational structures and interests. In everyday conversation these might be called "foundations" as a way of distinguishing them from federal funding sources. It is also possible that funding sources such as the American Cancer Society might be thought of as federal funding because they are so large. Knowing the differences among these sources is helpful in choosing the most appropriate funding source for your specific project. An important distinguishing characteristic for nonfederal funding sources is that they are not necessarily constrained to award funds within a specific period. This means that if no applications meet their standards, they can decide not to make any awards rather than fund the best of what they receive. We, like others (Dusek, Burke, & Kraut, 1984), find it useful to group nonfederal funding sources as follows:

- *National Voluntary Health Organizations.* The American Heart Association and the American Cancer Society are examples of national voluntary health organizations.
- *Foundations.* These include both public and private foundations. An example of public foundations are community foundations, which receive their funds from individuals, families, or companies. Private foundations generally fall into one of three groups: operating, corporate-sponsored, or independent.

The funding procedures of the voluntary health organizations and large independent sources are similar to federal sources—that is, they target specific program and funding areas and hire staff responsible for program and grant activities. In addition, some use a variety of funding mechanisms and special applications and can accommodate multiyear projects as well as those requiring large financial support.

Besides the considerations associated with the appropriateness of the funding source and the application procedure, a pitfall with private foundation funding is that the answers to the research questions may not coincide with the expected research outcomes. Using the alcoholic beverage industry as an example, Wallack (1992) indicates that the alcoholic beverage industry distributes millions of dollars annually for alcohol research. However, this research rarely comes to a conclusion that is not compatible with the interests of the alcohol industry (Montague, 1989).

National Voluntary Health Organizations

National voluntary health organizations such as the American Heart Association and the American Cancer Society have procedures similar to those used by federal agencies. They provide complete application instructions with their application materials as well as information about review criteria. These organizations provide financial support at a level similar to that of federal agencies, fund multiyear projects, and use a variety of funding mechanisms and special applications. There are some differences, however. The length and structure of the application might not replicate the Public Health Service application. Some applications, in fact, may be limited to as few as four pages.

These organizations use review procedures that meet their needs. Be aware that their review procedures may not mimic those of the federal government. The review group members might be scientists or nonscientists or a combination of both. Although every application should be free of jargon, it is more critical to be lucid and complete in your presentations for these organizations because of the possible heterogeneity of the review group. Most important, take their expressed mission seriously. These organizations have specific interests and will not fund projects outside those interests, no matter how compelling the presentation.

Public Foundations

Community Foundations. Community foundations generally restrict their grants to a prescribed geographical region, and perhaps only to the region where their offices are located. Therefore, if your research is not planned for the geographical region in which a foundation funds, however attractive the other aspects of the foundation are, do not apply. It should be noted that community foundations generally have limited funds and do not make awards for long-term projects or those requiring large financial support.

Private Foundations

Operating Foundations. Operating foundations generally conduct research with their own staff and, therefore, do not make awards. Occasionally, they seek assistance from those outside their organization to fulfill the program needs.

Company-Sponsored Foundations. Support for these foundations comes from profit-making organizations, but the foundations remain separate from those organizations. They fund specific areas of interest and make many small awards rather than a few large ones.

Independent Foundations. Most private foundations are independent. The Robert Wood Johnson Foundation, the Ford Foundation, and the Carnegie Corporation of New York are several of the larger foundations representative of this category. Not all independent foundations arrive at funding decisions in the same manner. Some do not have a formal procedure for receiving applications, although ultimately they usually require similar application information from the investigator.

Independent foundations can decide upon an interest area and seek research projects only within that area. For example, the 1991 annual report of the Carnegie Corporation of New York stated that

> the Corporation's grants are made for purposes that are broadly educational in nature. . . . the foundation makes it a policy to select a few areas in which to concentrate its grants over a period of years. . . . Currently the grant programs fall into three broad areas: The Education and Healthy Development of Children and Youth, Strengthening Human Resources in Developing Countries, and Cooperative Security. (p. 5)

The areas in which a foundation has an interest are discernible from its promotional materials, annual reports, and public relations materials. Although securing a list of projects previously funded can be useful, it is not as reliable as the other sources of information because changes in focus and interest occur periodically.

Independent foundations develop their own application review procedures. Some foundation review groups consist of academics, others of only foundation board members, and still others of a combination of academic researchers and community representatives. As with the national voluntary health organizations, it is advisable to anticipate a heterogeneous review group.

Business and Industry

In recent years the advantages of stronger bonds between business and industry and researchers in academia and community agencies have been recognized, and funds have become available for select research categories and community projects. However, applying to business and industrial organizations for these funds is very different from applying to the other organizations outlined in this chapter. One of the major differences is business and industrial organizations do not accept unsolicited proposals. Another major difference is the absence of people in program project staff roles. The importance of a contact person is not diminished, however, and the investigator must identify the individual who can best serve that role for the proposed project. For information on securing funds of this type of research and project support, read *Get Funded!* by Dorin Schumacher (1992).

SELECTING A FUNDING SOURCE

It is clear from the above discussion that the most effective strategy for selecting a funding source is using information about the source and its priorities. For example, the Diabetes Research and Education Foundation has a priority to fund research concerned with the "treatment of patients with diabetes," and the mission of the NIH has been to improve the health of the citizens of the U.S. If a research application submitted to either of these organizations is an exceptionally well-written proposal with meticulous attention to scientific method and analysis of results but does not meet the requirements of the mission statement, it will not be funded. Most funding sources cannot support broad missions such as funding good science; many do not support pilot, exploratory, or basic research with no foreseeable application; and some exclude medical research. Each funding source also restricts its funding in other ways. For example, many funding sources either limit or prescribe how awarded funds can be used, have eligibility criteria, or limit funding to specific types of projects.

A number of publications (Dermer, 1980) describe private foundations and their emphasis, and detail the types of grants available as well as the range of grant funding. A most useful place to begin exploring foundations as a possible granting source is the Foundation Center. The Foundation Center was established as a clearinghouse for private foundation funding to make grant information widely available (Kurzig, 1981). It provides information on foundations and is the direct source for anyone seeking information or an indirect source through its publications. Krathwohl's description of how to screen for foundation prospects (Krathwohl, 1988, pp. 214-221) should be reviewed by investigators who have never done a search and those who do not have an application support office staff to do the search for them.

The Grants Register is a source of foundation grants with an academic focus. It is updated every 2 years and lists seven kinds of assistance. Scholarships, fellowships, and research grants make up one category of grant assistance that is relevant for community agencies. Although a major source of state assistance to community agencies, service grants are not included in *The Grants Register.*

Selected Influential Funding Source Requirements

The following are some funding source characteristics and requirements we find useful to review when we seek a funding source.

Funding Source's Mission, Interests, or Priorities

The mission statements of funding sources often encompass broad objectives that cannot be reasonably met within a particular award period. Priorities, therefore, can vary from one award period to the next. This also means that review groups respond more favorably to some projects than to others, even though they may not rank them as high technically. It is our recommendation that the new investigator consider the congruence of both the mission statement and the priorities of the funding source with his or her interests when selecting a funding source. If there is no other information, guidance can be obtained from a list of the source's funded projects. But remember, current priorities may not be the same as past priorities.

Although the new investigator needs to find a funding source appropriate for the project's topic, the match need not be perfect. If you cannot find anyone with an interest matching the project you have outlined, consider modifying your plan so that both you and a funding source can get what you want. Remember our principle: Develop your questions first, then search for a funding source. It is also not a good idea to try to include every possible interest of the funding source in a single project application. When you have located a funding source that seems to have a compatible interest, get complete information about its funding policies, procedures, and review criteria. Selected resources for locating a funding source are listed under this chapter's "Action Strategies."

Funding Source Contact Person

Because not all funding sources have contact people, first determine whether a contact is available to respond to inquiries from potential investigators. Contact people can provide valuable information about the funding source's project and research preferences. Such information may be basic to the success of your application. For example, some funding sources require material, such as a letter of intent, before proposal submission, or impose funding limits which do not meet your project's requirements. It is a good idea to clarify your questions in writing before telephoning the contact person. Telephone conversations can take unexpected turns, and your list of questions will ensure that you ask all relevant questions and sound competent. Because your reason for making the call is to learn more about the funding source's requirements, have some idea about the kinds of materials you want to request. If you already have material about general objectives, request additional information that details their current priorities, objectives, and the required application materials. Be ready to answer questions about your project! After all, the reason for the conversation is to assist both you and the contact person in determining whether your project is within the interests of that particular funding source.

Eligibility

Eligibility requirements vary from one funding source to another. Therefore, determine that you and your organization are eligible. Remember, some funding sources only fund projects within a particular state, region, or city; award funds to individuals or institutions; require selected credentials for principal investigators; and place limits on the number of awards made in a single project area. You can avoid receiving a reviewer comment such as, "The problem has only local significance" or "The problem is not significant in our region" by carefully investigating funding source eligibility criteria before submitting an application.

Type of Project

Funding sources select the kinds of projects they will support. At any particular time, a funding source might fund basic research projects, evaluation projects, applied projects, training projects, curriculum development, and demonstration projects, or elect to fund only applied and curriculum development projects. This is an issue apart from the mission, priorities, and funding source interests. For example, a project concerned with crimes against children could be designed to fit into any one of these types. We suggest that the new investigator determine what type of project she or he wishes to have funded and apply only to those funding sources that fund that type of project. In our experience, taking the position that the funding source can be persuaded to modify its funding policy by a superior application most often fails to produce the desired results.

Application Deadlines

Application deadlines are usually stated in application materials. These might be either postmark or receipt deadlines, a distinction not to be overlooked. Choose a funding source with deadlines you think you can meet. In addition to application deadlines, some funding sources require a letter of intent or prefer to review a preproposal before receiving the final document. Deadlines for preproposals or letters of intent are often set well in advance of the proposal deadline. This means that considerable work must be done in a very short time to communicate the intent of your project effectively.

Project Period Restrictions

Funding sources often have a preference for the project's timeframe. Some funding sources prefer to fund only short-term projects. Thus if funding for 5 years is needed, do not apply to such a funding source even if the area of interest is similar. On the other hand, some funding sources are not interested in projects that require less than 3 years to complete. If your project is a short-term project of 1 year or so, you need to choose a funding source that supports short-term projects, and if you require 5 years you should apply only to funding sources that can support those projects.

Funding Schedules and Restrictions

Funding arrangements need to be compatible with your project requirements, your project timetable, and the regulations of your financial affairs office. Some factors to consider are the following:

— Earliest start date. If your research is season dependent, it is important to select a funding source that can accommodate your required start date.
— Regulations about the amount of indirect costs (overhead) allowed
— Maximum direct costs allowed
— Restrictions on direct costs by year
— Earliest possible funding date
— Option to extend research timeline if required, with unexpended funds
— Option to carry over unexpended funds from one research year to the next

Application Process

The application content is usually similar across funding sources, but you may need to attend to procedural differences. Therefore, information should be obtained about the project plan format, additional forms required, institutional approvals required (e.g., animal and human subject protection, drug-free status), and general guidelines that include information about type-size requirements, page length restrictions, and overall structure of the document.

Review Procedures and Criteria

Review criteria and procedures vary with the funding source. An important piece of information is the composition of the review group. Review groups can consist of university personnel or people from the community with a variety of backgrounds. The tone and style of a proposal need to address the particular configuration of the review board. However, in all cases a proposal must, to as great an extent as possible, be written in everyday language.

Information about the review criteria contained in the application materials focuses the composition of the final proposal. A copy of the instructions that the funding organization sends to its reviewers will assist in determining how some parts of the application are weighted differently than others as well as whether the criteria deviate from those you assume.

A copy of a successful application can be useful. It will give you an idea of what the reviewers are probably accustomed to seeing. Yours should have a similar appearance.

In summary:

• Learn the funding source's procedures for reviewing applications.
   Do scientists, laypersons or some combination of both serve as reviewers?

How is the funding decision made (priority score, selected agency personnel, family foundation board)?

- Study the review criteria.

What are the review criteria? They will guide the way you put the application together.

Are the parts of the application or project plan differentially weighted?

Request a copy of the instructions sent to reviewers, as well as the review criteria.

ACTION STRATEGIES

Sources of Funding Information

The Scientist. The Scientist Inc. (312) 762-2193. This periodical has a Profession section that includes news about both grants and grant makers.

The Chronicle of Philanthropy. The Chronicle of Higher Education. (202) 466-1234. This publication includes news of interest to both grant givers and grant seekers, including lists of grants awarded by nonprofit associations and foundations.

SCI/GRANTS News. IMV, Ltd. (800) 27-Grant. This publication focuses on grants that fund the purchase or improvement of equipment or facilities.

Federal Register. Superintendent of Documents, U.S. Government Printing Office, Washington, DC 20402.

Commerce Business Daily. Superintendent of Documents, U.S. Government Printing Office, Washington, DC 20402.

Foundation Center. 888 Seventh Avenue, New York, NY 10106. To order publications or a catalog, use their toll-free number, 800-424-9836.

NIH Guide for Grants and Contracts. Available from NIH Guide, Printing & Reproduction Branch, National Institutes of Health, Room B4BN23, Building 31, Bethesda, MD 20892.

Use Available Resources

The task of finding a funding source can be facilitated in most research universities by research development units and in community agencies by university faculty and consultants. These units and individuals can assist new and established investigators in locating funding sources as well as in writing applications and preparing budgets. We suggest that the new investigator discover resources and use them. Also available, either through the research development unit or from a funding source you choose, is information about the review process, including review criteria and characteristics of the review group. In addition, new investigators might seek out individuals and organizations in the business of providing consultation and training about the grant process.

Know the Mission of the Targeted Funding Source

Select a funding source that makes awards for the type of project you want to propose. Sometimes a funding source makes a decision to exclude certain kinds of projects even though it appears that they would be within its mission statement.

Contact the Funding Source

Contact the funding source to determine if there is a staff member in the program project officer role. If there is such a contact person, discuss any uncertainties you have about the match between your project and the foundation's current interests. Remember to prepare a list of your questions and try to get answers or directions to other people or places for the answers.

REFERENCES

Carnegie Corporation of New York. (1991). *Grants and appropriations 1991* (p. 5). New York: Author.

Dermer, J. (1980). *Where America's large organizations make their grants.* New York: Public Service Materials Center.

Diabetes Research and Education Foundation. (n.d.). *Grant research application.* Bridgewater, NJ: Author.

Dusek, E. R., Holt, V. E., Burke, M. E., & Kraut, A. G. (Eds.). (1984). *Guide to research support* (2nd ed.). Washington, DC: American Psychological Association.

Krathwohl, D. R. (1988). *How to prepare a research proposal: Guidelines for funding and dissertations in the social and behavioral sciences.* New York: Syracuse University Press.

Kurzig, C. (1981). *Foundation fundamentals: A guide for grantseekers.* New York: Foundation Center.

Montague, W. (1989). Brewers grants for research on alcohol issues prompt questions about objectivity of studies. *The Chronicle of Philanthropy, 1*(12), 1, 8-9.

Schumacher, D. (1992). *Get funded!* Newbury Park, CA: Sage.

Turner, R. (1986). *The grants register.* New York: St. Martin's.

Wallack, L. (1992). Warning: The alcohol industry is not your friend. *British Journal of Addiction, 87*(8), 1109-1111.

PART III

Research in the Real World

The Playing Board

8

Research Environments

This chapter focuses on the research environment. Research environments are defined here as settings in which data collection occurs or from which data collection is directed. Data collection entails a variety of factors and issues that differ from one environment to another. The collection of data at a remote site does not relax the requirements for project resources at the PI's location (the organization to which the award is made).

Investigators, without reflection, often behave as if all research environments are the same as their own. It is quite natural to assume that other investigators have as few or as many resources as we have and that research objectives are similar. Research plans are developed around the availability of resources. Funding sources often request information about the match between the research scope and content and the available resources. When investigators remain within their own group, department, or agency and within their expertise, the scope of planned research usually matches the resources available, and research objectives do not vary dramatically among project investigators. However, with the increased pressure for research to be multidisciplinary and multispecialty, it is often necessary to go beyond one's own location and reach beyond one's own area of expertise to develop a competitive research application. The purpose of this chapter is to high-light the variety of material and professional environments in which research is done.

It is tempting to try to classify research environments by their missions. This approach would categorize one group for academic research units, another for community organizations, and perhaps another for clinical settings. However, this scheme would not reflect the research components because wide variation not only occurs within each group, it also overlaps across groups. For example, the research capabilities of a clinical department in a College of Medicine may be more similar to those of a community organization than to the basic science departments in the same college. Thus it is important that the new investigator make no assumptions about the appropriateness of the research environment for a proposed project. Current information should be the basis for the development of the research appli-cation and the choice of the collaborators.

RESEARCH COMPONENTS

Data Sources

The most important characteristics of data sources are their reliability and availability, whether they be human, animal, paper records, or computerized data files. It is critical that no assumptions be made about these charac-teristics but that up-to-date information be obtained.

Humans

Depending upon the research data, human subjects could be students, in-patients, out-patients, or community agency clients. However, a point we would like to stress is that whatever your experiences have been with data collection from any source, you should assume that the situation has changed. For example, if your information is that 10 potential subjects appear each day at an agency, go to the agency and verify the information by collecting data over a 7 to 14 day period. If you are assured that patient records always include age, check the records to assess the extent of missing information and also the way age is recorded: Is it month, day, and year of birth, or is it reported age with no birth date? If you are told that access to certain populations is generally easy, do a walk-through of the system you plan to use in your research to observe how it works. Sometimes there is a perception that a system is efficient and reliable, but a closer look reveals that the people staffing the system are in fact the system and the key elements to its success. It is risky to assume that a system with this characteristic will be efficient and reliable in the future. A new investigator should be aware that accessibility of a data source can depend not only upon the formal system but also upon the personalities of those involved in making the contacts, either with the research participants or with those who manage the record systems. This variety of systems and personnel places a high premium on checking for reliability and availability when human subjects are required for research.

Animals

Everything said about human participants also applies to animal subjects. The additional factor with animal subjects is the animal suppliers. New investigators should talk about reliability of animal suppliers with investigators who have had experience with them.

Records and Data Sets

Records, either paper or computerized, are frequently a data source. Even though much data is computerized, do not assume that the data you need are computerized. Everyone is familiar with the work entailed in gathering data from paper records. However, computerized records are not necessarily more simple to access. The variety of systems, methods, and preferences of data technicians and programmers means that detailed information must be sought about computerized data just as it is sought about paper records. When you are told a database is available, get all the details, whether it is in-house or public. It could be computerized or planned to be compatible with your project needs, or it could be a nightmare for your project. Storage of computerized data sets also can vary from one installation to the next. For example, if the data are usually available on a CD-ROM, your installation must be able to use the CD-ROM or you must arrange to have the data transferred to a medium your installation can use. To reiterate, check data sources for reliability, availability, accuracy, and completeness.

Laboratory Space

Laboratory space is generally designed for specific types of work. If your project requires laboratory space and this part of the project is outside your area of expertise, spend enough time with the investigator associated with this part of the project so that he or she clearly understands the outcome you are seeking. If you hear things like, "Well, our lab isn't really set up for that kind of thing, but I think I can swing it," pursue further details. Inquire whether the project set-up would be done each time it is required, or whether the lab can be modified. Each of these alternatives has consequences that must be addressed in the application.

Clinical Space

Some research requires medical and physical examinations. If this is not your area of expertise, inspect the space your collaborator says can be used and question the fit of the data collection procedures to the space. Again, be alert for information that creates ambiguity about space availability. Keep in mind that if participants cannot be examined as scheduled, data collection will back up, and if other project components rely on these data, the whole research project can quickly grind to a halt. In addition, the custom for securing space for future use might vary across organizations. For example, in a particular unit, the custom may be to simply bid for the space, and when the time comes arrangements will be made. If you are not comfortable with this kind of informal arrangement, the first thing you might do is find out what "arrangements will be made" means. Perhaps what appears to be very informal is actually based on a more formal priority system. If that is the case, you can work with your collaborator to get a high-priority rating for your project. You might do some informal observations to determine how well the system works, or you might get another location and/or collaborator. What probably will not work is attempting to change a research environment outside of your own unit.

High Technology Instrumentation

The technology required for data collection covers a very wide range. If your data are to be collected by high-technology instrumentation, a thorough investigation of the availability of instruments is critical. This examination should include the scheduling procedures and the distribution of time across different projects. For example, you might require Magnetic Resonance Imaging (MRI). In this instance, keep in mind that not only the instrument but also the trained personnel are needed. It is important that you visit the facility and discuss your project with those who would need to be involved in sample preparation, instruction in use of the instrumentation, and data analysis. You should also check on availability for the time you expect to be collecting data, even though the data collection period may be at least a year in the future.

Computer Resources

Computer resources are basic to developing a competitive application and following through with the proposed research and data analysis. The heterogeneity of computing resources across research environments is surprising. However, do not assume that computer resources or computer skills are part of your collaborator's research environment.

Keep in mind that many computer resources are designed to meet specific needs. Therefore, although two research environments may both rank high on computer resources, they may not be compatible with each other. Ask potential collaborators about their computer resources, including word processing software and staff, statistical support software and staff, and electronic communications ability. Because electronic mail is becoming more common and for most purposes faster than a telephone call, availability is important.

Major Equipment

Major equipment is expensive. If you or your collaborator requires major equipment, determine whether it is in place or must be purchased. It is very important that a need for purchasing major equipment be recognized early because this type of purchase often requires a separate application. With shrinking research dollars, other funding sources for major equipment should be sought. Do not assume that major equipment is available because of its importance to your collaborator's work. Inquire about availability, condition, and age if cutting-edge technology is important for a competitive application.

Human and Animal Subject Protection

Organizations differ in arrangements with respect to human and animal protection. Some organizations accept approval from another organization and some do not. In the latter case, a research project must be reviewed by two or more groups. If you are in a location that does not have an Institutional Review Board (IRB), arrangements need to be made with another organization. Do not assume that you do not need review. Research procedures should be designed with the assumption that IRB approval is needed. Therefore, it is an advantage for an investigator to understand the IRB rules and the policies of the review board he or she will be following.

OBJECTIVES OF PRINCIPAL INVESTIGATORS
AND COLLABORATORS

Not only do resources vary across research environments, but professional objectives can also vary. Often individuals assume that everyone who does research has objectives similar to their own. This was once exemplified by an attempt of a practitioner and a behavioral scientist to collaborate. The topic of research was temporal mandibular joint (TMJ) pain.

During the course of several meetings, the practitioner and the behavioral scientist discussed data they would collect, data that would result in useful information about the syndrome, the kinds of patients available, the schedule for data collection, and the research design and statistical analysis. It seemed that both the practitioner and the scientist had the same project objectives. During the fourth or fifth meeting the behavioral scientist presented data forms and questionnaires for each patient to complete and discussed a schedule for each patient to visit the practitioner. The practitioner said, "We can't do this." Needless to say, the behavioral scientist was surprised and asked why. The practitioner replied that his primary concern was the well-being of his patients and that, in his opinion, the behavioral scientist would impinge negatively on his patients. The behavioral scientist made an attempt to dissuade the practitioner from his opinion but was unsuccessful, and the research was not done.

In our opinion, it is important to spend time getting to know a collaborator's expectations for a project. For investigators who have not worked across research environments, gaining this familiarity is particularly important because issues surrounding research expectations are not insurmountable. However, we do see one area of research that is particularly prone to problems—evaluation research.

Evaluation Research

Evaluation research has expanded as a direct result of demands for accountability in resource distribution. Although evaluation research uses a full range of research methods, it is often a political undertaking (Cronbach et al., 1981; Jones, 1985; Weiss, 1972). When programs compete for funds and have constituencies reliant on their services, conflicts of interest can arise. For example, program directors and evaluators, and evaluators among themselves, might see a program in entirely different ways. The early surfacing of differing expectations about project objectives permits time to develop a plan for accommodating the differences.

The Evaluator as Evaluator

It is critical for the community agency to incorporate a viable evaluation when developing a competitive application for applications that require an evaluation. On the basis of our experience, one issue that is important to a community agency selecting an evaluator is making an application competitive with a strong evaluation and a strong protocol that must be weighed against the ability of the evaluator to work with the staff of the community agency after funding is received. We have found that this issue can be a major area of discomfort for both community agency staff and the evaluator.

The evaluator's role should be defined at the earliest opportunity in the application development process. We also believe that the evaluator should be involved in the application development process and not involved only through a late afternoon telephone request on a Friday a couple of weeks before the submission deadline. Contacts with researchers and evaluators should not be one of the last steps in preparing the application, no matter how much the investigator dreads making the contact.

For the evaluator, a last minute contact and request to develop an evaluation protocol means there is little lead time or face-to-face contact with community agency staff. In addition, the evaluator is given limited opportunity to discuss the planned project and the evaluation protocol. Thus the community agency does not make good use of the evaluator's expertise in shaping the project, refining the application's content, or fine-tuning the design and evaluation protocol. Consequently, the later the contact is made with an evaluator, the more likely there will be significant problems with the application, specifically with the relationship of the evaluation section to the overall application.

Because one of the authors is involved in drug and alcohol research, we would like to use a recent experience as an example of the importance of timing when selecting an evaluator. During the past 2 years we have been contacted several times by community agencies with the specific need to develop an evaluation protocol for examining the effectiveness of an application for an alcohol and drug service demonstration grant.

These evaluation needs are part of an application that the community agency will submit to the Center for Substance Abuse Treatment (CSAT) or the Center for Substance Abuse Prevention (CSAP). In their grant announcements, CSAT and CSAP specify the evaluation protocol as a required component. The targets of these demonstration grants that provide treatment and prevention services or expand services are specific groups of alcohol and drug abusers or groups at high risk for alcohol and drug use. These demonstration programs, as outlined in the grant announcements, require both process and outcome evaluation. According to the most recent grant announcement available when this chapter was written, 15% of the total demonstration budget of these grants are to be committed to process and outcome evaluation activities, and evaluation is to be an integral part of the application.

It has been our experience that review committees seem to favor outside evaluations rather than agency-based evaluations for these demonstration grants. These evaluations are to focus on examining the effectiveness of specified goals and related targeted objectives that are generally directed toward reducing the incidence and prevalence of alcohol and drug abuse within an identified and targeted population or geographic area.

In our encounters, contact by community agency staff seeking to meet evaluation requirements is most frequently made by telephone and is sketchy in defining needs and content. As stated above, evaluations need to be developed quickly to be part of a grant application. Most frequently, written materials are limited or unavailable to the potential evaluator for use in developing the evaluation protocol. On the basis of our discussions with other evaluators, these experiences are common and seem to vary only slightly with other community agencies and service providers who are seeking evaluation expertise.

It has also been our experience that evaluators are most frequently identified by community agency staff through word-of-mouth contacts. As an example, for a recent demonstration grant submission deadline, one of the authors was contacted by five different community agencies who were preparing CSAT and CSAP demonstration grant applications. Two of these applications focused on high-risk youth with problem behaviors, two applications focused on addicted women and their children, and the remaining application focused on an intervention for addicted women. The applying community agencies represented five separate communities in three states: Kentucky, Kansas, and Ohio. When the agency staff members were asked how they had heard about the author, each of them replied with essentially the same answer: "We heard about you from a friend, and he or she said that you evaluate community programs and have helped get funding." Thus word gets around—this fact is not new—but it needs to be restated here because there may be a limited number of evaluators in whom community agencies believe they can place their "trust" and who have been successful in helping community agencies get funding for demonstration projects.

We believe the principles of trust and confidence that are presented here are important ingredients for community agencies. In other words, the evaluator has no axes to grind and no predetermined notions of evaluation findings or outcomes. An example comes to mind: A researcher who was very interested in carrying out research in prisons and targeting women's issues recently contacted one of the authors. After only a short discussion, it became obvious that this researcher was not only interested in the research area but also, and probably more important for the setting, had an interest in issues related to feminine and personal rights. After further discussion it appeared that the real issues were masked and that study findings and the interpretation of data would be most interestingly shaped by the researcher's biases. This became a dilemma for the host setting in which the research was being carried out (apparently not a new issue for community settings that have research opportunities).

The Evaluator's Role for the Community Agency

Ask community agency staff members about an evaluator's role, and they will probably respond by saying that their role is to see whether something works. When pressed, most respondents will add something about the development of information related to the efficiency and effectiveness of a project, and this is related to resource allocation and funding. This can be an evaluator's role, and an examination of processes (i.e., how many people are served) and outcomes (i.e., changes in the behaviors, attitudes, values, and opinions of those involved) must be undertaken to determine when the stated project goals and objectives are being achieved. Although oversimplified, the evaluation role of an impartial data collector with responsibility for analyses and report preparation is not always the case but it is traditional.

Evaluation Roles

An evaluator can assume different roles. Some of these roles can be traditional, whereas others can be focused with more intense involvement. The principle for the community agency to keep in mind is the importance of knowing which role is needed to make the application's evaluation most competitive. The evaluation and the evaluation design can range from very invasive, with randomization of service recipients to different kinds of service and control groups, to a more participatory and hands-off role with the collection of qualitative data with participant observation.

A Researcher May Not Be an Evaluator

An issue for community agency personnel is the following: What you see is not always what you get when it comes to research and evaluation. It is important to use that thought and to keep in mind that a university or other researcher may not be an evaluator. In other words, there are different and distinct kinds and levels of research protocols and evaluation approaches. These differences are manifested with the kind of research design and thrust. An evaluator is most likely to examine a project's ability to achieve stated goals and objectives, whereas a researcher may be more interested in theory development and hypothesis testing and/or continuing his or her line of research. Talking with the researcher/evaluator about his or her interests is the most important way to understand this issue. Studies that address both issues can frequently be carried out.

ACTION STRATEGIES

The following action strategies are grouped into two areas. The first set of action strategies provides guidance for community agencies to use in selecting a demonstration project evaluator. Emphasis is placed on the situation in which an evaluator is needed if a community agency is to be competitive for the review process and subsequently for funding and project implementation. A second group of action strategies is presented to assist researchers, who may not be evaluators, in selecting community agencies to carry out their research.

That these motivations are distinct and different is often not recognized by a number of persons who are interested in community organizations. On the basis of our experience, these needs are usually different. In addition, situations can become confusing and frustrating for both parties if these separate, but compatible, motivations are not understood. This can be further complicated by the fact that community agencies often feel threatened by researchers and evaluators, even though the uneasiness is not verbalized. Perhaps this goes back to the days of the efficiency expert who looked over a worker's shoulders, or maybe it is related to the fear of possible criticism and uncertainty. Whatever the motivation, we wish to emphasize that these feelings are real and can dampen the overall goal of carrying out community-based research and evaluation. With that background, the following action strategies are presented for community agencies.

Action Strategies for Community Agencies to Use in Selecting an Evaluator

The following action strategies can be used to assist community agency staff in selecting an evaluator. The need for agency evaluations, as stated above, is usually in response to a funding source requirement for evaluating a specific project that is part of a grant application or a contract proposal. Thus this need is usually related to external funding requirements.

Knowledge About Grant or Contract Requirements

Remember that a grant application is different from a contract proposal. A grant application outlines an approach that responds to a broad grant announcement. A grant announcement outlines broad objectives that we described in Chapter 3. A contract proposal, on the other hand, is a response to a particular scope of work that is usually very specific in project requirements and consequently in evaluation requirements. A contract is developed to meet the funding source's specific needs. For example, states and counties contract for construction projects such as building roads and highways. For our purpose here, a contract outlines the project's services parameters and the evaluation requirements in a most detailed fashion, with limited room for creativity on the part of the community agency and the evaluator.

Thus, the kind of evaluation design required in a contract will be very targeted, detailed, and described in the request for proposal. This is the kind of research and evaluation activity in which fewer academics seem to have interest. However, this is an important evaluation need for a community agency in preparing a contract proposal, and it is crucial for a community agency to clearly outline this need when interviewing and selecting an evaluator.

Locating an Evaluator

An important issue for community agencies seeking grant or contract funds for projects that require evaluation is to select an evaluator who can meet the evaluation need specified in the announcement or request for proposal. In other words, both evaluation expertise and substantive expertise are needed to successfully compete for the project and then to carry out the evaluation as part of a successful project. These requirements may not be mutually exclusive, but they are frequently found in different people. From the point of view of a community agency, it seems that the evaluator should meet both needs. Subject matter expertise and evaluation skills should be linked within the same person, and this is the most favorable and frequently the most productive way of accomplishing the project's goals after successfully competing and obtaining funding.

It seems most logical that evaluators can be contacted through a local university. However, we have learned through discussion with community agencies that this is not always easy to accomplish. A number of factors appear to effect the availability of university-based researchers and/or evaluators. A most important factor is the availability of time to carry out an evaluation or research activity. In some cases it is most important for university-based faculty/evaluators to become involved in community activities as part of their community service. However, academics may be involved in other projects and not be available. Faculty may be interested in supplementing their salaries with funding from a community grant and/or contract funding and can be most interested in involvement with community agencies. It should also be noted that some university faculty are interested in specific areas of practice and the related research, and they look forward to working with community agencies.

There are also university centers and institutes that bring together researchers and evaluators in order to target activities in specific areas of interest, depending on the university. These university groups can be most helpful in meeting community agency needs for research and evaluation. After a university center, institute, research group, or faculty member is located, it is important to do some homework and checking before contact.

Ask About the Evaluator's Track Record. This point appears to be obvious. However, we discovered this the hard way in one of the evaluations in which we are currently involved: Questions need to be asked. The university-based evaluator who was contacted to develop the evaluation plan for a demonstration project learned after funding that his evaluation protocol was not acceptable to the federal funding agency. The evaluator, from what we understand, would not modify his evaluation plan, and the fun began for the community agency. Rather than making modifications, both the federal agency representative and the evaluator dug their feet into the ground. Soon there was a suggestion that unless modifications were made, there was a chance that funding would be discontinued, and this was enough to make the community agency take notice.

After asking around the community, the community agency, which is geographically distant from our university, asked us to carry out the evaluation to alleviate the problem and meet the evaluation requirements that, in the eyes of the funding agency, could no longer be met by the proposed evaluator. Thus we have been engaged in a geographically distant evaluation protocol, which would seem somewhat illogical if this background is not understood. We were selected after the agency asked around about availability, and were accepted on the basis of past experience and through a previously established relationship with the community agency.

Plan Ahead. The need for planning is critical if a community agency is to have adequate time to shop around for an evaluator who fits the community agency's application needs and to have adequate lead time to develop a well-thought-out application in concert with the evaluator. Early contact also provides lead time for the agency to integrate the thoughts of the evaluator into the evaluation. If these thoughts are not integrated or discussed so that the evaluation approach is modified, the application will be weaker and will be less likely to be approved by the review committee. The following suggestions will lead to a better understanding of the qualifications of evaluators and researchers.

What Is the Evaluator's Experience With the Subject Area?

The evaluation plan will be strongest if both the community agency and the evaluator have experience in the area being considered. That is why pilot studies are important for a research proposal. The same is also true for demonstration applications. For example, when investigating or researching the drug and alcohol area, it would seem logical to contact experience evaluators to develop and incorporate their resumes in a demonstration evaluation. However, the application would not be as competitive if the substantive area were early childhood development. However, sometimes we must use what is available, but it is best to know that the decision is being made explicitly and with thought.

Ask Questions

One of the best recommendations we can make is to suggest that the community agency staff ask questions and ask them continuously. If the answers given do not make sense in light of the project that is planned, then modifications need to be made during the application development process. Following the trail of external funding can be exciting, but after approval and funding are received, do not forget that the project must be carried out within the parameters of the application and the evaluation design.

Action Strategies for Researchers to Use in Selecting Community Agencies for Their Own Research

Community agency-based research has included control/comparison designs and has been fairly invasive. However, and more recently, there has been an interest by the Substance Abuse and Mental Health Services Administration and other federal agencies in services research. This interest by Congress and others has helped establish a new agency in the Public Health Service that focuses on services research and follows more recent congressional needs for applied research to better understand what works best and for whom. The following action strategies are presented for researchers to use in contacting community agencies so they can carry out their own research in those settings.

What Experience Has the Agency Had With Evaluation?

On the basis of our experience, it is important for a researcher to ask pointed questions about the professional experience that agency personnel have had with research and evaluation. Most frequently, their experience was part of their undergraduate and graduate education. Usually that experience, which was either neutral or more often negative, was largely dependent upon circumstances and motivations. It is interesting to note that the most successful evaluation protocols with which we have been involved in commu-

nity agencies as evaluators were in those agencies with the most motivated
staff to carry out research.

What Data Are Available?

Clearly one of the ways to determine whether a community agency has
research and evaluation interest is to ask about the types of data it collects and
how the data are used. It has been our experience that asking this question is
very important because the response usually is a good indicator of research
interest. For example, a community agency that does not use an automated data
system can be very different from an agency with a system in place. It might also
be important, from a research perspective, to use the automated data system,
but the point we are trying to make is that a data system is a possible indicator
of the agency's research interest and commitment.

Do Agency Personnel Use Research Findings?

Another overall indicator of a community agency's commitment to research is how agency staff keep current with practice or the approach that is
usually used. In other words, what kinds of data are used, and how do
individuals keep up with the literature and research findings? It seems
obvious that agency staff who attend conferences are interested. Other
indicators include "journal club" activities to discuss research findings,
in-service training, and didactic supervisor practices. Another overall indicator that has surfaced is the positions taken regarding research and the use
of research findings by the agency board of directors, if there is a board, and
the agency executive director. We have come into contact with a number of
community agencies over the years, and the agency research climate is most
important not only for using research and evaluation findings but also for
initiating research projects.

Are There Possibilities for More Rigorous Designs?

Talking with the agency director, board members, and staff is a direct route
to determining the agency's research climate. As part of that temperature
measurement, we suggest that there should be discussion related to exploring rigorous designs. What do staff think about randomization and comparative designs? What about the idea of providing different levels of intervention? If a waiting list exists, could it be used as a control group? Is it
acceptable for staff to deliver a standardized, manual-driven intervention?

In summary, we believe that community agencies can provide a viable setting for carrying out services and demonstration research as well as research planned by academic and other investigators. We recommend that relationships with community agencies be opened after specific issues are examined and discussed in a straightforward manner. Developing an application or proposal can be an exciting experience if properly planned, or it can be a series of ongoing problems that are almost unsolvable.

REFERENCES

Cronbach, I. J., Ambron, S. R., Dornbusch, S. M., Hess, R. D., Hornik, R. C., Phillips, D. C., Walker, D. F., & Winer, S. S. (1981). *Toward reform of program evaluation.* San Francisco: Jossey-Bass.

Jones, R. A. (1985). *Research methods in the social and behavioral sciences.* Sunderland, MA: Sinauer Associates, Inc.

Weiss, C. H. (1972). *Evaluation research: Methods of assessing program effectiveness.* Englewood Cliffs, NJ: Prentice Hall.

9

Relationships and Interactions

This chapter introduces the complex area of human relationships and interactions. The focus here is not on all relationships but on those we believe are important if potential investigators are to be successful in developing a competitive application. Although the first part of the chapter is concerned with relationships and interactions in general, the second part focuses on selected professional contacts and relationships. We believe that each contact is important for the new investigator. Contacts made while developing project ideas and applications can grow into relationships that foster continued professional collaboration.

PRESENTATION OF SELF

In a professional context, there are no contacts with others that can be considered "throwaways." They all count. Whether the contact is by telephone, FAX, e-mail, letter, manuscript, scheduled meeting, coffee-shop meeting, seminar, hallway meeting, research application planning meeting, or just a passing "good morning" in the corridor, we each leave an impression. In the instances where contact is face-to-face, impressions are based on what is said, how it is said, and body language. How we dress, smile, frown, stand, walk, and sit communicate a lot about us, leave impressions, and can even override what is said. Consider the kinds of impressions others make on you. The first thing you probably notice is that what catches your attention changes from day to day. Some days you seem to be ranking everyone on organizational ability; another day it might be on the style of dress or the degree of expressed vulnerability or dependency. The same person, on different days, might leave a different impression.

We also leave impressions on people with whom we have not had contact through the impressions we make on those with whom we have had contact. These secondary impressions can be a very important foundation in the building of networks. People try to collaborate with those who have reputations for being positive and actively engaged in intellectual pursuits. We repeat: All contacts count. You cannot be sure which dimensions others will focus on, but you can attempt to leave good impressions about your competence, efficiency, orderliness, accuracy, and creativity. Impressions about your professional life are made in conversations, your attire, the neatness of your work, and your general deportment. However, you do not always want to make the same first impression. The impression you want to give collaborators when you are the PI on the project application is different from the impression you want to make on your mentor or someone from whom you need assistance. The impression you want to give collaborators is that of being knowledgeable, organized, in control of the project, and open to discussion of ideas. The dominant impression you want to make on someone from whom you seek help is that you are teachable.

When you are searching for project colleagues, you will hear many impressions of potential candidates. Always consider the source of these impressions—the person relaying them to you may have values different from yours. It is also not always possible to meet collaborators before project development begins. However, whenever possible, you should meet potential collaborators and form your own impressions of how they meet both your personal and professional requirements.

One of the principles we present in this chapter is that an investigator, in reaching beyond and outside his or her immediate area of expertise and social environment, must accept responsibility for learning something about other professional communication styles and behavioral patterns because the manner in which we present ourselves becomes more relevant under these conditions. It is our belief that applications that cut across disciplines are desirable and are now being funded. An example of this trend is the 1993 National Institutes of Health (NIH) announcement of the Interactive Research Project Grant (IRPG). This collaborative funding mechanism was developed by NIH to focus on certain biomedical and behavioral research questions that extend beyond the single project or require a variety of technical approaches beyond the means of the single investigator. The IRPG program encourages the coordinated submission of related project grants (R0-1s) that share a common theme, are tightly focused, and describe the need for project linkages.

Conversational Skills

Conversational skills are an important component of interactions and relationships. Everyday politeness goes a long way in most brief interactions connected with developing a project application. Do not hesitate to ask questions. Learn how to ask questions directly, without prefacing them with, "This is probably a stupid question. . . . " A bright person is not knowingly going to ask a stupid question. A bright, teachable person knows there are very few stupid questions. If you do not understand the answer, say that and try to get the answer in another way. When a topic has not been thoroughly discussed in a multidisciplinary setting, it is sometimes difficult to know how to ask a question so that the intent is understood. In this situation it might be useful to state the problem and let your information source help phrase the question. When you are the information source, exercise patience and understanding with colleagues who are struggling to learn about and use the language of your area of expertise.

Develop conversational skills that open communication channels and keep them open. Use jargon only with colleagues who also use it. Try not to be abrupt. Some people expect to engage in small talk before "getting down to business." Accommodate them when you can. You may hesitate to call some people for information because you know that the small talk might go on for as long as 5 minutes—more time than you care to devote. One solution is to not call until you have a long list of questions, so that the 5 minutes prorated over the number of questions is a reasonable expenditure of time. Learning to initiate conversations with people you would like to meet enables you to meet potential collaborators whenever opportunities arise. One way to initiate such conversations is to simply approach the individual and say, "Hello, my name is Tom Thompson. I just read your article in the _ journal about _. I found it quite helpful in my work." This statement lets Tom Thompson know what you know about him, and it also tells Tom Thompson something about you and your work interests. When others attempt to initiate conversations with you, respond in a way that suggests additional conversational topics. A single word response such as "yes" or "no" without elaboration might be taken as a cue that you are not interested in pursuing the interaction.

Develop habits that keep communication channels open after contacts. A habit of distributing minutes of a meeting within 24 hours after the meeting is a good way to convey your interest and appreciation for help to group members. If you ask a colleague to critically read a document, express your appreciation. It does not take much of anyone's time to show appreciation, and it keeps at bay the label of "user."

Work at identifying miscommunication. An example of miscommunication is given by Bobbert (1992, p. 3). One time he asked a young secretary to type a letter for him. She said, "I don't care to!" He did it himself and was angry about it. Later he learned that what she meant was, "I don't mind doing it." This kind of miscommunication is very possible when a group of people with training in different disciplines and from different work settings collaborate on a project application. If the response you receive seems unusual, try to verify what you understood. Among potential collaborators a few minutes of seemingly redundant conversation is preferred to a miscommunication that could affect the success of a project application.

Collaborators and consultants are standard components of most project applications. Whenever you meet someone with whom you can discuss your research and your ideas, stay in touch. If it is someone in your own organization, a telephone call now and then or a coffee break together keeps you both apprised of what is going on. If you have met someone from another city at a national meeting, write a letter or send an e-mail message after you get home letting the person know that you enjoyed the interaction. Keep in mind that not everyone is a regular user of e-mail. If you routinely use e-mail, let others know this and ask whether they prefer to use it or regular mail, telephone calls, or FAX. Keep in mind that FAX and e-mail are not appropriate for private communication.

COMMUNICATION ISSUES

Two communication issues are so basic and pervasive that they are often overlooked as areas that require special attention when developing a project application. The first, which has received some attention, is gender.

Gender

Not all that long ago, men talked with men and women talked with women in many project areas. Now, men must talk with women and women must talk with men on almost all projects because gender no longer parallels disciplines and areas of expertise. Men and women must communicate effectively within areas of expertise and disciplines as well as across them.

Tannen (1990) raises relevant issues in her book *You Just Don't Understand: Women and Men in Conversation*. Tannen suggests that men and women live in different worlds, so conversations can be likened to cross-cultural communication. She indicates that from early childhood, girls play with a best friend or in small groups and use language for confirmation and to reinforce intimacy. On the other hand, boys use language to protect their independence and to negotiate status in large-group activities. These patterns continue throughout adulthood. Hence women and men can come away from the same discussion with very different interpretations of the conversation and will most likely have very different interpretations of discussions and meetings focused on application development.

Tannen's (1986, 1990) books, which discuss communication issues across gender and cultures, have raised consciousness about interactions. Now, more than previously, it is acceptable to reflect on what people say and ask questions when something is not clear. Sometimes you may find yourself saying, or hear someone else saying, "Oh, *that's* what that is!" Thus questions and reflections about what is heard are important for productive and enjoyable exchanges.

A second communication issue frequently overlooked is communication openness. Most people probably agree—some more than others—that open communication should produce a better application. We believe that open communication is very important for developing competitive applications and implementing projects.

Open Communication

Some people use information to enhance their power. This is usually done by withholding information until it can be used to the holder's best advantage. The hope is that everyone working on an application will provide all relevant information in time for the final draft. But systematically withholding information can, in our opinion, be destructive for both the application development process and for project implementation.

Men and women have historically held different meanings for open conversation (Tannen, 1990). But with the raising of consciousness about gender differences in communication style, it is not wise to assume the character of a conversation on the basis of the stereotype. Some ways to prevent communication problems are to provide information, distribute written minutes to all group members after each meeting, entertain questions, be responsive to feedback, and be diplomatic but straightforward about your thoughts on the project. These are logical methods and are what meaningful relationships are made of. At least these are techniques to try. However, science is not apolitical, and all scientists do not value each other's work. In this environment, some maneuvering is inevitable as each participant seeks to learn how he or she can exercise control. No templates can be used by new investigators to successfully navigate these kinds of storms. Becoming an acute observer of shifts between open and closed communication that are specifically and strategically planned can be helpful to the new and the seasoned investigator. Watching a mentor navigate the stormy waters is also an effective way for new investigators to learn how to successfully work with colleagues and collaborators during project development.

Chapters 5 and 6 discussed formal and informal resources available to PIs. Most of the time, access to these resources requires communication with others. Some of these contacts will develop into relationships; others will remain at the level of repeated interaction. Note the word "repeated." Even though contacts do not always develop into relationships, politeness and understanding remain important.

POWER

Power is a variable that, as most people understand in a general way, operates in many situations. In our opinion, it is important for the new and the seasoned investigator to consciously consider the importance of power and its use when developing an application. We have observed that new investigators who have had difficulties in establishing workable relationships have frequently been hindered by their misunderstanding of the use of power and have not grasped the importance of recognizing power in every context. The importance of power must be recognized and thought through. Once power is understood it can be used appropriately. We suggest that a new investigator should spend time thinking about power in its relationship to the project application and devise procedures for successful negotiation.

What Is Power?

Power has been defined in many ways. One of the ways it has been defined can be paraphrased as the amount of influence one person has over another. This influence can flow from personal power, position power, performance power, or perceived power.

A combination of performance and perceived power is an attribute a new investigator seeks in collaborators. These types of power are derived from the expertise that an individual has developed and for which he or she receives professional recognition. This type of "powerful person" is the kind of person the new investigator may seek out to not only add "power to the application," but also for the work that is needed. In other words, power as used here is not hierarchical but is related to the expert's knowledge, either real or perceived. This type of power can be the cause of thoughtful and, at times, not so thoughtful planning when collaborators are considered necessary for an application. In our experience, this seems especially true when collaborators are sought from other universities, because of the absence of recent performance information. For the new investigator, this combination of power is highly valued, especially when the needed expertise is directly related to enhancing an approach and is thought to significantly increase the competitiveness of an application.

Another type of power is legal or legitimate power that is organizationally sanctioned and is frequently related to one's position in an organization. This type of power can be described as legitimate power, on the one hand, or as the kind of power a supervisor has over his or her subordinates, on the other hand. Depending on personalities, this type of power can be helpful, or it can be a major hindrance in developing a competitive application and implementing the subsequent project. In our opinion, it is important to assess the power relationships and to govern your behavior accordingly.

COMMUNICATION HETEROGENEITY

We have come to the conclusion that relationships with collaborators must be established to achieve a successful application and project. We also believe that these relationships can be very different, depending on personalities and settings, and can be one of the most complicated and unrecognized areas requiring attention as the new or seasoned investigator prepares an application. However, there appear to be limited absolutes because some things work for some investigators whereas other investigators indicate that certain principles are most unrealistic. We also believe that an individual's position and organizational power are highly associated with collaborative relationships and can easily complicate communication and possibly preclude joint activities and projects. We believe that relationships and communication are to a large extent personality driven and organizationally bound. For example, we cannot remember the number of times investigators have said to us that they are unable to work with a colleague even though the relationship would be to the advantage of both for preparing the application.

Open communication plays an integral part in preparing an application, and we have observed complicated difficulties when communications have gone awry. These "cross-communications" lead to misunderstandings. For example, what is acceptable in an academic environment of pointed and directed questioning may be severely criticized in a community setting because this style is most likely to be considered hostile. It is, therefore, important to recognize differences that exist between an investigator's host setting and those of collaborators. Recognizing differences is important, but urges to make substantial modifications to either environment must be resisted. We would argue that avoiding controversy is best, and we believe that time and energy are best focused on the application. In our discussion of principal investigator qualities in Chapter 1, we suggested and encouraged a personal and professional strategy that is open and available to all collaborators. We believe that such a strategy is currently used by successful principal investigators, particularly those who sustain their projects over time. We will suggest several approaches that can be useful in specific situations and make suggestions for explicitly examining the importance of these approaches when establishing relationships.

MULTIPLE RELATIONSHIPS

The effective investigator is successful for a number of reasons that complement the investigator's scientific knowledge. One of the key reasons for success is the ability to form relationships with multiple individuals, including those identified below.

Other Investigators

Other investigators may be the keys for a successful application, especially in the current funding environment that encourages cross-disciplinary research. It is easy to recommend establishing cross-disciplinary relationships and sometimes easy to accomplish. However, sometimes establishing relationships that incorporate both needed scientific expertise and commitment is difficult to achieve. For example, one of the authors is currently the co-principal investigator on a center grant funded by one of the National Institutes of Health. This center grant cuts across disciplines and sectors of the university. During the weekly scientific and administrative meetings, more time than we thought necessary was focused on understanding the particular details of each study and the specific techniques and components. We soon discovered that we were engaged in learning scientific applications and techniques as well as different meanings for different concepts. What we also learned is that theory and models can be most helpful in understanding research approaches.

Community Agencies and Organizations

Community agencies and community organizations are host settings for research, particularly behavioral research. We have found that certain community organizations have a tradition and culture of being comfortable with research. That tradition is usually historical and related to the organizational leadership. Thus a principle to keep in mind for researchers interested in becoming involved with community research is to simply ask about those community settings that have a research tradition. It is also important for the community agency to ask about university researchers, their research history, and how they "handled" controversial findings (Leukefeld, 1989). It must also be noted that certain community institutions are skeptical of researchers because of the controversy and hidden agendas that might play out in a research project. Finding community connections may be important if some investigators are to be successful.

Practitioners

Developing relationships with practitioners and practitioner groups can be a research avenue for the new investigator. It has been our experience that most successful practitioners are interested in "what works," and many practitioners have opinions that can be quickly focused as testable hypotheses. In fact, we have discovered that once the word gets around that a university professor is willing to work with practitioners in developing evaluation protocols, contacts are made for a variety of protocols. However, we have also learned that this takes developmental time and commitment on both sides. In addition, we have discovered that the initial contact, usually by telephone, is the best time to understand expectations. Practitioners, like the rest of us, are pressed for time to meet deadlines, and they usually wait until it is critically important to make contact for the evaluation. Consequently, if the timetable is too close, it is important for the potential evaluator to say that the design can or cannot be developed. If it can be developed, it is important to indicate that the design details and background may be weak. Thus the practitioner recognizes that important contingencies need to be considered in developing the project, and may wish to consider submission at a later time because a fundable project cannot be developed with the necessary detail in such a short time.

Collaborators and Consultants

You may be asking, "How are collaborators different from other researchers?" We have in mind individuals who are positioned to help get the application approved. Some applications refer to these kinds of people as consultants. Others are included as collaborators or "substantive experts," usually from out of town, who will enhance the application with their expertise and knowledge. As an example, we recently developed an application to reach injecting drug abusers in rural areas. We knew from the outset that it would be very difficult to convince the review group of the opportunity to carry out research in rural America, where HIV prevalence is low, and of the ability to implement the study in such a rural area. What we did, among other things, was to involve a consultant from another university who had carried out funded HIV research in rural areas. He had moved "to the big city" and had thought about rural areas and his commitment but had not found collaborators. So we joined together for what we considered the best of both worlds, and his involvement, advice, and expertise, which helped us get a very good peer review as well as a funded application.

Subjects

It may seem strange to include research subjects as important factors for developing relationships. But we have discovered that most successful researchers pay particular attention to subjects and do not label them "subjects." The important benefits of becoming involved in a research protocol can go beyond the incentive(s) given. One of the authors participates with colleagues in a longitudinal evaluation study of a federally funded drug abuse prevention intervention in a remote area. Although incentives are provided, we discovered something that seems obvious now: Our visits, which involve collection of both quantitative and qualitative data, are becoming more personal as qualitative and personal interview data are collected. We mutually update key informants about the various activities that have been part of our lives since our last visit. These updates become important for both parties, and the content of these relationships seems to be meeting personal needs for study participants. In instances where communication with subjects beyond data collection is not possible because of its possible influence on the data, the interactions between subjects and investigators should still be polite and attentive.

Budget Officer

A critical relationship that needs to be maintained is with the new investigator's organizational budget officer and, if available, those people who process grant applications within the investigator's host organization. These people can range from someone in an office who has responsibility for officially signing the application, along with the principal investigator, to a person who can help prepare the application budget on a spreadsheet. A close working relationship, in our opinion, helps forestall the inevitable problems that are associated with funded project budgets and the changes in them that usually take place. Having someone who can help interpret rules, policies, regulations, and customs is something we have found to be critically important.

Obviously, we have been selective in the number of relationships we have described here. Others, including organizational administrators or managers, have sanctioned responsibilities for reviewing applications in certain organizational environments. Boards and community groups can also have real or perceived "review authority." And, finally, competing persons and organizational units can expend time and energy in dampening proposed projects because they perceive those projects as being in their domains.

NEEDED EXPERTISE—AT WHAT PRICE?

Some potential investigators have a wide range of contacts, whereas others, especially new investigators, will most probably have few. What we would like to suggest is that multiple possibilities for establishing relationships will be beneficial for preparing an application. What we are not suggesting is that the potential investigator should "hang out" in certain areas without a plan. But we are suggesting that the new investigator take time to selectively establish targeted contacts that can be beneficial for ongoing relationships. We suggest that decisions about relationships should be made explicitly rather than without thought about both the positive and negative aspects of establishing relationships. The cost of compensating for negative aspects of a relationship should be assessed. A reasonable cost is specific to the project, and often it is difficult to find models for guidance of what an unreasonable cost might be.

ACTION STRATEGIES

The following action strategies are presented to enhance the new investigator's ability to develop competitive applications with the goal of strengthening relationships. We clearly have not identified all possible areas that might present relationship difficulties. However, we believe that the following areas cover important strategies that we have observed and they are presented for the new investigator to consider.

Communication Breakdown

Remember, communication breakdown occurs under the following three conditions (Bobbert, 1992, p. 17):

We don't really say what we mean.
What we think is not what we say.
People hear what they want to hear.

Agreements Made During Project Development

It is our suggestion that certain agreements need to be made during the application development phase of the project. If these agreements are completed, they will facilitate relationships throughout the project development phase and during project implementation. Difficult situations can be avoided if there is agreement at the outset and if this agreement is renewable. Some of these agreements are put into writing, whereas others need only be discussed, depending on personalities. We believe that keeping minutes and distributing the "points of agreement" to participants will go a long way in avoiding difficulties. It should be noted that avoiding relationship difficulties and focusing on prevention may not be easy during the planning phase but is invaluable for the project's success when it is funded. Open discussion should be encouraged at the very beginning to bring out trivial issues that can grow into mountains very quickly. Keep in mind that "open discussion" does not always look the same; it is a function of the PI and her or his collaborators. If meetings are going well and a group is productive, don't worry if it doesn't operate like the "open discussions" of another group.

The Principal Investigator as Captain or Royalty

The PI must take the leadership role in preparing the application as well as in orchestrating the application activities after the application is funded. The PI sets the tone for the meetings and the expected level of energy. For example, it is a mistake to believe that a good impression will be made by opening a meeting with excuses about how busy you are, how little sleep you have had, and how your car has finally really let you down. Open communication does not demand that you share this information. If you are in this situation and you cannot conduct an organized meeting, it probably would be best to cancel the meeting. People are generally not tolerant of poor performance excused in this fashion, and you will no longer be at the starting gate but far behind in your efforts to develop a competitive application.

The PI's leadership and management style directly influence the tone of the research group. Over the past several years there has been discussion and often times debate related to the benefits of different leadership and management styles. We will not enter that debate here, but we would like to suggest that participatory management styles can lead to more productive use of time. However, that is not to say that the potential principal investigator should not have an idea and be prepared to describe that idea in detail. We are reminded of meetings in which participants were ready to join the application process, but no one took the leadership role and directed the process. Participants soon got frustrated, and we recall a meeting in which one participant asked, "Why don't you just tell me what you want me to do so we can get on with it?" Timetables can frequently be used as a neutral mechanism for accomplishing this end. However, a timetable can only be used after fundamental agreements have been worked out. The principal investigator is responsible for the project but may take very different approaches to participatory management, something about which the co-investigators should ask during the application development process.

Program Official

Program officials can, and in our opinion should, be contacted throughout the application development process. The National Institutes of Health model describes the program project officer as follows:

> Functions include responsibility for monitoring, providing technical assistance and reviewing the project relative to all scientific, technical, and programmatic aspects of the project. (NIH Grant Award Letter, 1993)

It is important to consider the advice received—especially if it is advice from a funding organization's program official—although it has been our experience that most of us more readily accept the advice with which we agree. But it is also important to use this consultation to circumvent possible difficulties related to project changes and/or modifications.

However you feel about the advice given, or if you perceive a negative rather than positive attitude, resist the impulse to form a "we/they" attitude.

The program official is bound to relay organizational rules and policies. It is important to be polite and empathetic if you wish to get maximum assistance. If you don't like a particular piece of advice, investigate whether it would change if you presented a slightly different circumstance. Say "thank you" and let the program official know that you appreciate her or his efforts on your behalf. Build a "we" association. Remember that old saw, "Two heads are better than one."

Grants Management

The funding source grants management officer, or fiscal/budget officer, is the person responsible for all budgetary items and fiscal accountability for funded projects. The grants management specialist, in accordance with the National Institutes of Health model, does the following:

> Functions include responsibility for the business administration and management of the project and the resolution of nonprogrammatic questions including the applicability of Public Health Service grants policies. (NIH Grant Award Letter, 1993)

In our experience, it is important to check with, and in most cases receive approval from, the funding source budget official before changing budget line items or modifying a project budget.

It is important to treat this person, and/or the representatives of this person, with respect. This, like all interactions, is not a "throwaway" encounter. This recommendation again seems obvious, but several colleagues have not understood this. And in our opinion, they have endured needless site visits and/or the most limiting interpretations of guidelines for their projects because of the truncated relationship they established with grants management officials. Remember, these people are responsible for completing the paperwork to cut the yearly checks.

Publication Authorship and Sequence of Authorship

For academics and those interested in advancing the state of knowledge, it is important to discuss both possible publications that may result from the project and collaborators' publication roles. From what we have seen, this can be a major issue and a problem for collaborators after funding. It seems logical that the individual who has the most expertise in a procedure or approach should be the lead author on resultant publications. However, this may not be the case because the principal investigator may command control of all publications. The principle we present here is that it is appropriate to discuss authorship as part of the initial application process so that there are no surprises. We have been involved in collaborations that have had no discussions about the publication process and in those that have established written procedures for authorship during the project's planning phase. From our observations and experience, we strongly recommend publication discussions during application preparation.

Timetables for Completing Work

We will suggest in Chapter 12 that a timetable be developed when preparing the application. A timetable for the project implementation, agreed upon by the collaborators, is also useful to help guide relationships after an application is funded. This timetable can be sufficiently detailed so that it can be used to direct the project and serve as a focal point for discussions, which are frequently avoided because difficult issues are easy to avoid. Do not mistake a casual nod of agreement for commitment to complete a particular piece of work by a particular date. Whenever we ask someone to do something, we are negotiating for their time; the negotiation is not complete until the date and time for completion of the work have been agreed upon. With a timetable in everyone's hands, the constraints of the funding source are visible to all investigators.

Financial Considerations

A variety of financial issues must be considered during the application development phase and after funding. An important consideration for the applicant institution is the indirect costs paid by funding sources. These established rates are a percentage applied to the total direct costs. There have been discussions about the federal government placing "caps" on the indirect cost rate to control project costs. Indirect costs of 40% or more of direct costs are frequently perceived by investigators as a burden on project costs. Other financial issues include salary savings for the investigators. These savings could be used differently within organizations and can include support for research, equipment, heat, light, and telephones through fiscal resources that can be used to enhance an investigator's work. In some settings, incentives as percentages of the total award are made available to investigators for additional research. In other words, a variety of financial issues can be associated with funded projects. We suggest that the new investigator ask about his or her organization's funded project policies and traditions.

Do Co-Principal Investigators Get Credit?

An important point to consider is the amount of credit that a co-principal investigator will receive for being part of a successful application. Part of the involvement is learning about the process with a goal of becoming a future principal investigator. This is no small point, as we have discussed elsewhere. However, other project benefits should be addressed as part of the initial discussions related to the co-investigator role. Sometimes principal investigators tend to forget that co-investigators are not students and have established themselves in their own right. Therefore, it is our suggestion that those things of particular value for the co-investigator be negotiated at the outset. In academic settings, this can range from primary authorship for specific analyses to managing certain aspects of the project protocol.

Mentoring

One of the traditional ways of learning about relationships in academia and business is through mentoring. Selecting a mentor is important for several reasons, including the potential insight the new investigator can receive about relationships and the relationships needed to develop a successful application. In our experience, the desire to be competitive has brought new investigators to our doors only because they have heard that we had assisted others in a supportive way with their applications. This was how we have established mutually satisfactory relationships with pre- and postdoctoral researchers, and we highly recommend it.

Interpersonal Skills

It is not uncommon for new investigators to feel uncomfortable with the multiple interpersonal situations they will confront as a potential PI. Negotiating skills are important in achieving goals and in appreciating the ubiquitousness of negotiation. Setting priorities can be seen as negotiating with ourselves. Getting along with difficult people is another important skill. Keep in mind that someone with whom you have difficulty is not necessarily a problem for others. How often have you heard, " . . . but my experience has been very different"? The following references might be useful:

> Fisher, R., Ury, W., & Patton, B. (1991). *Getting to yes: Negotiating agreement without giving in.* New York: Penguin.
> Solomon, M. (1990). *Working with difficult people.* Englewood Cliffs, NJ: Prentice Hall.

Learn What You Can About Other Areas of Expertise

Sometimes, something as simple as a dictionary can be useful in acquainting yourself with another area. The following have been found to be useful:

> Seplaka, L. (1991). *Concise dictionary and handbook of economics, finance and statistics for health care.* New York: Professional Horizons.
> Vogt, W. P. (1993). *Dictionary of statistics and methodology: A nontechnical guide for the social sciences.* Newbury Park, CA: Sage.
> Yaremko, R. M., Harari, H., Harrison, R. C., & Lynn, E. (1986). *Handbook of research and quantitative methods in psychology.* Hillsdale, NJ: Lawrence Erlbaum.

REFERENCES

Bobbert, L. C. (1992). *Don't talk! Communicate!* (pp. 5, 17). Kingsport, TN: Printing Concepts.
Leukefeld, C. G. (1989, November). Evaluating programs in health care settings. *Health and Social Work, 14,* 231-234.
NIH Grant Award Letter. (1993). [Personal communication to Dr. Carl Leukefeld].
Tannen, D. (1986). *That's not what I meant! How conversational style makes or breaks your relations with others.* New York: William Morrow.
Tannen, D. (1990). *You just don't understand: Women and men in conversation.* New York: William Morrow.

PART IV

What and When to Write

Rules of the Game

10

Research Details

What to Write

This chapter discusses the components of the research plan and provides suggestions for each of them. An application is divided into several components that together and separately should give the reviewers a balanced and focused understanding of the project. The basic components of your research plan are the following:

Title
Specific Aims (Objectives)
Background and Significance (Literature Review)
Preliminary Studies
Experimental Design and Methods
Abstract
Literature Cited

TITLE

It is common to overlook the power a title has to direct or misdirect a reviewer's attention. Carefully crafted titles communicate effectively and guide reviewers' expectations. We believe that the following are some of the characteristics of a good title:

- Good titles are short.
- The first word categorizes.
- Good titles are interesting.
- Good titles are informative.

Good Titles Are Short

Short titles are preferred because they quickly communicate the application topic. They do not express complicated relationships. In some instances, as with the NIH guidelines, application instructions limit the number of characters and words permitted in a title. However, we have seen titles that are two lines long, containing as many as 20 words. For example, "Prospective Comparative Analysis of Psychological Response of Patients Undergoing Immediate Breast Reconstruction Following Mastectomy Versus Mastectomy Alone for Breast Cancer," is too long and complex. A better title would be: "Breast Reconstruction: A Prospective Psychological Analysis," but even with this title some ambiguity remains about the research focus.

The First Word Categorizes

The first word is important as a categorization tool because funding source staff members frequently group applications by using the first word. Sometimes this sorting is done by hand, which allows for making judgments based on the entire title rather than on a single word. However, computer sorting is now sometimes used and most likely will be used more in the future, placing a premium on first word precision. In the title, "Prospective Comparative Analysis of Psychological Response of Patients Undergoing Immediate Breast Reconstruction Following Mastectomy Versus Mastectomy Alone for Breast Cancer," the proper categorizing word is the fifth word ("Psychological"), but it could also be the 11th word ("Breast"). The authors of this title clearly wanted to be certain that reviewers were immediately aware of both research and design highlights—too large a burden for a title. It is important that the title include the most important features that differentiate your research plan from others, and is particularly important in order for research grant applications to avoid the adverse consequences of having the application reviewed by an inappropriate review group.

Good Titles Are Interesting

An interesting title is informative, not catchy. Use of slang, synonyms, or analogies is not appropriate in application titles. For example, the title "Popping Pills: Prelude and Periodicity" is catchy but does not convey detailed information about the project plan. The information conveyed is ambiguous because the pills could be prescription drugs, over-the-counter medications, or illegal drugs. An interesting title presents the heart of the project plan in a way that provokes intellectual curiosity.

Good Titles Are Informative

It should not be necessary to search through the abstract, the introduction, or the first few pages of an application to determine "what it is about." The title should reveal important aspects of the project. Again, this requires investigators to precisely express the important research features. Titles will necessarily be ambiguous about some aspects of the project. For example, if a project uses adults as subjects and the distinction between adults and children/adolescents is important, the gender of these adults may not be specified in the title. On the other hand, if all subjects are men, then the word "men" must appear in the title, not "adults." It should also be noted that using "adult men" is redundant and only adds to the length of the title without adding information. In summary, an informative title sets up expectations for what the reviewer will find in the project plan.

Some words and phrases evoke stereotypes. The first two words in the title "Drug Use Among Physicians" suggest three different research projects. One is founded on the premise that physicians are using drugs for recreational purposes, another on the premise that physicians are overprescribing or underprescribing drugs to themselves or to patients, and still another on the premise of legitimate drug prescription by physicians. Be aware when composing titles, therefore, of the stereotypes that words and word combinations convey.

SPECIFIC AIMS SECTION

The specific aims or objectives section is an expression of the PI's research goals. The most effective presentation of these goals is to state them at three levels of generality: the broad long-term goals of the research area, the specific aims of the proposed research, and the hypotheses or questions generated by the specific aims. An optional element of this section, but one we think important, is a brief statement of the project rationale. In general, limiting the specific aims to one single-spaced page or less is a good idea. This length is usually sufficient for a concise statement of the specific aims and places a premium on tight writing because it does not allow for unnecessary digression.

For some research it is possible to state, in a list, the overall or long-term objective followed by the specific aims and the hypotheses or questions. However, it is our experience that a combination of lists with brief discussion paragraphs provides more information for the reviewer and is also a familiar presentation format for many principal investigators. The following is a discussion of what to include in each of the four components of the specific aims/objectives section of an application.

Brief Rationale Statement

The purpose of a brief statement of the rationale for the research is to provide information about the current conditions or positive consequences of the proposed research—in short, to set the context for the project. This might be done, for example, in terms of costs incurred by unsolved problems, contributions to scientific knowledge, or perhaps the need for research data that can be used to inform intervention strategies. Although the literature review section should present this material in detail, a brief statement early in the plan can deflect incorrect inferences on the part of the reviewer. Because one of the characteristics of a successful application is that it presents original research, it must be assumed that the investigator's line of thought and reasoning will not be immediately obvious to other scientists. Whether research contributes to scientific knowledge or applies current knowledge to new populations or to previously hidden problems, a rationale statement placing the research in its context relieves the reviewer of the task of reconstructing the PI's train of thought. Placing the research in a context also helps reviewers ascertain the significance and relevance of the research objectives to the mission of the funding source.

Broad Long-Term Objective

The overall long-term research objective is the broadest use of your findings. This objective can be reached only through extensive research by you and other investigators. Two tendencies are usually encountered by new investigators when they attempt to write this objective. One tendency is to have the objective encompass an area too broad and the other is to constrain the objective too narrowly. The universe of discourse for the long-term objective needs to be broad enough to justify the research efforts, yet narrow enough so that the applicability of the research to the final achievement of the objective is clear. For example, a broad long-term objective of improving the quality of life for all children in the world is too high a level of discourse for a research project concerned with health services for children in Appalachia. A broad long-term objective of improving the health of children in rural America is at a more appropriate level of discourse. The characteristics of the second example (improving the health of children in rural America) and of appropriate broad long-term objectives in general are the following:

- the objective cannot be achieved with one research project;
- the objective generates a variety of pertinent specific aims with accompanying hypotheses;
- the objective can be achieved through a series of investigations over time as each investigation either provides answers to some of the questions posed or enables formation of new testable hypotheses; and
- the objective is not stated as a hypothesis because it is not a relationship to be tested.

Specific Aims

Specific aims or research objectives are statements about the research outcomes. Specific aims are at the level of discourse immediately below the broad long-term objectives. These are statements of the problem to be solved, or how the project's findings will be used. These statements are not hypotheses; they are not tested; they are not descriptions of the methods through which outcomes will be achieved. For example, "The aims of this research are to divide the rural population of Kentucky into Appalachian and non-Appalachian groups and to survey the parents in each of these groups to determine health care needs" is not a statement of specific aims—it is a statement of the data collection methods. Specific aims are statements of the research accomplishments. The line of thought might be something like this:

> The broad long-term objective is to improve the health of children in rural America. It seems that the health care needs of children in rural America are not being met through the present health care delivery system. Part of this issue is the health care of rural children in each state. The problem in my state, presented as the most general question, is, "What is the relationship between the health of rural Kentucky children and the health care delivery system?" Therefore, if it is determined how health care needs are met and what the unmet needs are for rural children in Kentucky, I will be able to assess the extent to which the health care delivery system and health care needs mesh. My outcome measures will be indicators of barriers. Therefore, the specific aim of this research is the following: to determine the barriers to health care for children in rural Kentucky.

This specific aim is within the scope of the broad long-term goal. It is a statement from which several hypotheses can be generated, providing reviewers with the context for the hypotheses that are to be tested and within which data will be collected.

Hypotheses or Questions

Questions or hypotheses should have their origins in a knowledge base, and that base is presented in the research proposal. Do not form hypotheses on the basis of an investigator's comment, "It would be interesting to see what happens when variable X is included." The inclusion of variables in hypotheses or questions should be supported by theory or experience. Kerlinger (1964) points out that hypotheses must express a relationship and be testable. They must include, therefore, at least two measurable, or potentially measurable variables and their relationships. The choice of stating formal hypotheses or using questions depends upon the research. Hypotheses or questions direct the project's research design and the data collection methods.

In summary, the Specific Aims (Objectives) section of the research plan then includes the following:

- *Rationale*: A statement placing the research in a context that clarifies importance and urgency.

- *Broad long-term objectives:* A statement that assures that the investment in the research will have enduring value. It is recommended that the first part of this statement be, "The broad long-term objectives of. . . . "
- *Specific Aim(s):* Statements that address issues about which hypotheses can be generated. It is recommended that the first part of the specific aim(s) statements be, "The specific aims of this research are. . . . "
- *Hypotheses or Questions:* Statements that direct the project's research design and data collection methods.

The following instructions for the Specific Aims section are included in the U.S. Public Health Service application packet PHS 398:

> List the broad long-term objectives and describe concisely and realistically what the specific research described in this application is intended to accomplish and any hypotheses to be tested. (PHS 398 [Rev.9/91], p. 20)

LITERATURE REVIEW

The purpose of the literature review is to make a case for the practical or theoretical importance of the proposed project. The literature review demonstrates your understanding of the subject matter and justifies the need for the research.

An exhaustive literature review is neither required nor desired. Present only the literature pertinent to your project in a thoughtful and integrated way. The literature review needs to be written in a manner that persuades the reviewer that you have a solid grasp of your subject matter and that you read research articles with a critical and integrative attitude. The literature review provides an opportunity for you to show that you know science is not a collection of facts, but a search for an explanation and understanding of those facts. The following are the three suggested elements of this section: rationale for the research, theoretical position (if appropriate), and review of research inspiring the current project. The order of presentation of these components within the section will vary with the subject, discipline, and preferences of the principal investigator. In general, if each hypothesis or question presented in the specific aims has a literature, it is recommended that the literature review follow in the same order as the hypotheses or questions.

A book that might be useful in overcoming some obstacles encountered in writing the literature review is Cooper's (1989) *Integrating Research: A Guide to Literature Reviews,* even though it is directed at writing review articles rather than literature review sections within articles.

Research Rationale

This section amplifies the rationale for carrying out the research presented in the Specific Aims section. The literature review pertinent to the rationale should play a role in determining the importance and urgency of the proposed research. Present enough information to provide a complete context. However, refrain from mentioning every article that has ever been written. We recommend that you do not simply present a list of referenced facts and figures but rather write your own conclusions based upon the data and the relationships among them. Do not expect the reviewers to draw conclusions—state them. Be sure to include statements of how your proposed research will influence the current situation. The selection of articles is a demonstration to the reviewers of your ability to critically analyze and integrate material into a concise summary.

Theoretical Position

If your research is based on one or more theories, these theoretical positions should be briefly discussed. Carefully outline the links between the theories and your research. A clear discussion of the scientific rationale is imperative. Draw out the relationships between your hypotheses and the theory. Do not discuss a theoretical position and then never refer to it again. The theoretical development of relationships between cultural components and other research variables is uneven across disciplines; therefore, evidence that cultural influences have been considered is necessary for research involving minorities or subpopulations. Reviewers look for evidence that potential confounding of cultural issues with experimental treatment or intervention effects has been considered. For example, if a behavioral science research project uses people over 65 years of age as subjects, a discussion about the effect of socialization on the outcome variables might be germane.

Review of Research Inspiring the Current Project

An investigator reads as much of the literature relevant to his or her topic as possible. The reviewers, however, have no interest in reading abstracts of all of these articles, nor the details of each study. Your knowledge will enable you to write a concise and effective review of the material directly related to the project variables—not only to write words but to communicate thoughts. A literature review frequently progresses from general background information, such as early studies and early theory testing through amplification studies emphasizing either populations or variables, to current research that has sparked your interest and subsequently your research. We suggest that you include general background information, information about the trends that have been established, and a description of the customary research and statistical methodology. As your brief historical description of the research becomes more current, give greater attention to changing methodology (particularly if you propose to change it), sample size (especially if sample sizes are small for the type of research), and research design. The studies for which you need to provide the most detail are those that surround the gaps you propose to fill or the conclusions you are proposing to test.

In some areas of investigation, such as randomized clinical trials and others using experimental designs, investigators use quantitative literature reviews. In these reviews, data from previous studies are pooled and analyzed. This technique, called meta-analysis or CI (combination of information) (National Research Council, 1992), might be used in conjunction with a qualitative review. Its use, however, must be governed by the conventions of the research area and the composition of the review group. Unless a new investigator would be considered remiss for not including a quantitative review, he or she should seek advice from colleagues before including it as a part of the application literature review.

The literature review must be focused. Ruthlessly exercise discipline to exclude excursions into related research areas. Reviewers do not care about the breadth of your knowledge or about how many different topics catch your interest. Their interest is confined to what you include about the proposed research and how you think about the stated objectives.

Be selective in choosing the articles cited. We emphasize that you should not cite every article that makes a particular point. If several scientific leaders make the same point, state the point and use combined references. A sentence such as, "Evidence that this is the case can be found in several research reports, the most impressive of which are. . . . " might be used. Be certain to cite current research, and whenever possible, include research done by review group members. The literature review for intervention research should include a discussion of the efficacy of the intervention and the effective use of incentive strategies for retaining participants throughout the study.

The objectives specified set up expectations for the literature review. Reviewers may be perturbed when they do not find an expected literature, or find the literature in a list rather than in an integrated, persuasive, form that leads to justifying your research as the next step. You developed your research objectives after a careful and objective review of prior and current research. Therefore, we suggest that you state your conclusions and the related research in a straightforward manner. Although some of the research gaps you propose to fill have been rooted in inappropriate designs or statistical analyses of previous research, do not fan the flames of scientific controversy. Nothing is to be gained from tearing apart another's research in a research application.

A word of warning about using research carried out by review group members: Because the review group consists of investigators interested in research topics similar to the one you are proposing, it is reasonable to assume that some of their research is relevant. This is the research you must not fail to mention. However, if you cite research that is not relevant, the author (who is now the reviewer) will certainly know that better than anyone and may penalize you for it. However, relevance is not always as apparent to others as it is to us. Thus it may be important to discuss the criteria used for determining relevancy of included research findings.

The following summary presents these points from the U.S. Public Health Service application packet PHS 398:

> Briefly sketch the background to the present proposal, critically evaluate existing knowledge, and specifically identify the gaps that the project is intended to fill. State concisely the importance of the research described in this application by relating the specific aims to the broad long-term objectives and to health relevance. (PHS 398 [Rev. 9/91], p. 20)

PRELIMINARY STUDIES

The purpose of the preliminary studies section is to provide reviewers with evidence of your ability to do the kind of research you are proposing.

Write this section so it states the relationship between your prior work and the proposed project and also documents how your previous project experience will be used in the proposed project. The information in this section will help inspire confidence in reviewers about your experience and competence to pursue the proposed project. List the titles and complete references of appropriate publications and manuscripts accepted for publication.

Presenting pilot data for the proposed research is most helpful. Briefly describe your research projects that lay the groundwork for the proposed study. Keep in mind that you are not reporting the entire study as published, but you are summarizing those highlights that buttress the reviewers' perceptions of your ability to carry out research in a specified area with specified subjects, using specified methodology and data retrieval instruments. As in the literature review, avoid a seemingly endless list of research titles, procedures, and data. Present a carefully edited, integrated account of your previous research experience in the areas of the proposed research.

Because the Preliminary Studies section recounts prior work required for the successful conduct of the entire proposed project, not just that which is the responsibility of the PI, work of the co-investigators should also be included. Again, decisions must be made about what to include and what to exclude. Keep in mind what you are attempting to do. You are building a case to document that you, the PI, and your co-investigators are successful, competent, and knowledgeable in the area of the proposed project.

If complicated instrumentation is required, provide evidence that pretests have been conducted and that backup support is available should instrument failure occur. For example, if electronic or photo imaging is used for data collection, describe in detail the procedures you have used and report the reliability of your measures. Details are particularly important in instances where subtle changes in the position of the patient (subject) influence the image and consequently the data.

EXPERIMENTAL DESIGN AND METHODS

The experimental design and methods section describes the experimental design, procedures, and statistical analyses to be used to accomplish the project's specific aims. The section includes the components of a research article: experimental design, subjects, instruments, procedures, and statistical analyses.

Experimental Design

The design, experimental or other, must be clearly described. A statement that a "split plot" or a "regression discontinuity" design will be used is not sufficient. Some designs are unique to a discipline or a research area, and designs used in common across disciplines may have different labels. Therefore, it is helpful to the reviewers to describe the design in a way that clearly demonstrates its applicability to your hypotheses. In experimental or quasi-experimental research, comparison or control groups must be given as much attention as the experimental or intervention group(s). It is critical to be able to determine the effectiveness of the research manipulation. Carefully outline your rationale for choosing a particular group as a control or comparison group. In general, simple designs are preferred.

Subjects

Describe relevant characteristics of the subjects. Specify the ways in which the characteristics of the subjects and the sample that will be selected are appropriate for testing your hypotheses. Include information about projected attrition rates and, if significant, the corrective procedures you propose to use.

When human subjects are to be used, describe in as much detail as possible your expectation for including minority groups and/or women as subjects. Include data on minority rates in the population from which you will draw subjects and your recruitment procedures for minority and women subjects. Include oversampling plans whenever the proportion of minorities in the population is low and whenever oversampling does not invalidate your conclusions. If your research cannot accommodate minorities or is gender specific, discuss the reasons.

When research requires exclusion criteria, do not merely state them in general terms, but provide an operational definition of how the criteria will be applied. For example, if individuals with cerebrovascular or cardiovascular complications are to be excluded, give detailed information about how the presence of the complications is determined and the range of measurement values used to exclude potential subjects. It is often necessary to use samples of convenience. When this is the case, the significance of the method of subject selection for data interpretation should be discussed. It is important to defend the appropriateness of the sampling procedure, in spite of shortcomings.

Data Collection Instruments and Data Characteristics

Describe the data collection instruments, including reliability and validity information when appropriate. If you have selected one instrument rather than another, or have not upgraded an instrument, describe why the one you selected is appropriate for the proposed project.

The range of technology used for data collection continues to expand. If data collection uses cutting-edge technology, or technology that has not previously been used in data collection, greater effort must be made to describe how the collected information will become the data on which analyses will be carried out and from which inferences will be drawn. Be wary of using data collection instruments that are one step removed from the outcome variable. For example, the pill bottle with the electronic cap that records each opening of the bottle cannot be used as evidence that a subject has taken medication; the only measurement provided is the frequency of cap removal. This type of measure can be used, but it needs to be corroborated with an additional independent measure. The outcome measures for intervention evaluations must also be carefully chosen and must relate to the intervention rather than to the idiosyncrasies of the intervention participants.

Provide information on the measurement level of the variables (i.e., nominal, ordinal, interval, or ratio) and the type of scaling, (i.e., dichotomous, polytomous, or continuous). For some research, it is rare that all variables are continuous. Therefore, indicate those variables that are measured continuously, those that are dichotomous, and those that are polytomous. If you have information about how the scales are usually handled statistically, include that information. For example, some polytomous scales are routinely analyzed as if they were continuous.

For data collected over time, both short-term and long-term data collection procedures should be justified. A discussion of the adequacy of data collection over the short term provides reviewers with your rationale for data collection over a brief period. When data collection extends over a long period (e.g., several weeks, months or a year), a discussion of the strategy for providing incentives for subjects to remain in the study should be included. Also discuss the effects on the data of repeated meetings between the investigator and the subjects. For example, if it is considered negative for data to be a function of investigator-subject familiarity, procedures for circumventing this occurrence must be outlined. Although it is common in longitudinal studies to use the same data collection instrument on multiple occasions, discuss both positive and negative effects for your study.

Do not mention collection of data that will not be analyzed. The amount of work expected from each subject is called "respondent burden" and is a concern of many reviewers. Thus it is advisable that only data directly related to the project be collected. This communicates to reviewers that you have a solid grasp of the research parameters and do not wish to burden your subjects with excessive data collection procedures. An impression that you are collecting data on everything remotely associated with your topic can be detrimental to the final review outcome.

Procedures

Describe the proposed data collection procedures in sufficient detail for reviewers to understand them in general terms. "A telephone survey will be conducted to collect data on. . . . " is not sufficient detail. In this case, describe the interviewer training procedures, their instructions for entering respondent replies, and the hot deck procedures. "Participant observation will be used to collect data on. . . . " is also not sufficient detail. The label "participant observation" is one of many labels applied to procedures that invoke a plethora of details for those familiar with them but provide very little information for those in other disciplines or those familiar with other research procedures. Although the description need not go into microscopic detail, it must include enough detail so that someone unfamiliar with the procedure could duplicate the major aspects and imagine the data collection environment.

If there are alternative procedures in the literature, indicate the ways the procedure you selected is most appropriate for your purpose. If there is a possibility that something can go awry, discuss it and present the alternative action you will take. Particularly vulnerable to modification are participant recruitment procedures. These procedures have a direct effect on the composition of the proposed sample and need to be designed so that the final results are not biased. Reviewers are interested in the details of the planned procedures, especially if they entail oversampling, and in any modifications should planned procedures prove to be inadequate.

Whenever data collection requires training for data coders or interviewers, present a careful description of the training procedures and of the trainers' credentials. The detail required is dependent upon the uniqueness of the data collection methods. If there are standard practices, the description can be brief and referenced; otherwise, include sufficient detail to assure reviewers that training will be adequate.

In some research, data collection is associated with the occurrence of an event, such as the death of a spouse or the first visit to the physician. In these circumstances, a careful discussion of the appropriateness of the timing of data collection is imperative.

Data Management

Describe how you plan to record initial data, enter them for data analysis, and store them. It is critical that data entry, retrieval, and storage be given serious consideration because some data entry and storage systems are more vulnerable to data loss than others. Whenever possible, include a detailed description of your system and the factors that its design accounts for, such as research procedures and staff work style. When data confidentiality is an issue, detail the procedures you will use to ensure confidentiality without compromising data integrity. If you plan to use a data management center, include its credentials in the application.

Statistical Approach or Methods of Analysis

This section describes the statistical approach and related data analyses. Describe the statistical approach in as much detail as possible. The data analysis section should include descriptive statistics, data checks for outlying data with a discussion of how outliers will be handled, and data transformations you expect to use, such as log transformations. Present the specific statistic to be used rather than the most general label. For example, indicate the kind of correlation coefficient (e.g., Pearson's r, tetrachoric, or polyserial) or the kind of factor analysis rotation (e.g., varimax or promax).

The greater the complexity of the statistical analyses, the more important it is to include detail and to discuss the rationale for the analyses. Care with regard to these discussions communicates your ability to contend with whatever statistical problems might arise. Because statistical tests are used to test the hypotheses generated by the specific aims of the research, associating the statistical tests with their specific aims and hypotheses is extremely helpful to reviewers. The threads tying statistical tests to hypotheses are not always easy to follow. By spelling out the associations carefully, misunderstandings can be deflected. The same issues arise when multiple data sets are analyzed. Discuss the results you expect and how they will be interpreted.

Statistical Power

Statistical power is the ability of a statistical test to detect the effect size of interest. An important piece of information for reviewers is a section indicating that the sample size you have chosen is sufficient to detect a meaningful effect size, given your statistical design. Include the alpha level you have chosen, the effect size you want to detect, and the estimated standard deviation. When your analysis requires a variety of comparisons among groups requiring several statistical tests, include information on statistical power for all the major analyses.

Research Timeline

A research timeline describes the timeframe for the research procedure presented in the research plan. This timeline needs to be realistic! If only 2 years are allowed by the sponsor and the research requires 2 years, report writing will need to occur after the funded period. Start-up time is routinely underestimated. Although it is common, a serious underestimation of start-up time may generate uneasiness for reviewers about the conduct of the entire project. Therefore, we suggest that you do not underestimate the importance of carefully calculating the time involved in this phase of the project.

The research timeline is also a template for what is presented in the budget, year by year. The timeframe within which data collection occurs dictates the data collection expenses for each year. We suggest that you pay careful attention, therefore, to the availability of subjects or other data sources year by year and the feasibility of collecting data on all those available.

PROTECTION OF HUMAN AND ANIMAL SUBJECTS

Although it often appears that investigators pay attention to the protection of human and animal subjects only after an application has been submitted, that is not so. The criteria for the protection of human and animal subjects must be met within the research procedures. The following are some of the issues that will influence research procedures and selection of subjects for studies using human and animal subjects.

Human Subjects

1. Subjects must be identified by age, special population characteristics, and health status when relevant to the research. Gender and racial composition need to be considered, with careful consideration given to the inclusion or exclusion of any subpopulation. If subjects are members of vulnerable groups such as fetuses, pregnant women, children, human in vitro fertilization, prisoners or other institutionalized individuals, the rationale for the research must be sufficiently powerful to warrant use of the subjects.

2. The data source must be clearly outlined, as must statements of whether the data will be obtained specifically for research purposes or whether use will be made of existing sources such as specimens, records, or other previously collected computerized data (e.g., public data sets).

3. Recruitment plans and the procedures for obtaining consent need to be clearly described. It may be difficult to get consent from potential subjects. The difficulty might stem from their inability to read or sign their name on the consent form, or from the fear that consent will lead to their identification. The ability to obtain consent impinges directly upon the viability of the research and is, therefore, of critical importance to reviewers.

4. The risk of being a research subject needs to be considered and procedures must be developed to minimize the risks, whether they be physical, psychological, social, or legal. The research rationale must make clear that risks, when they exist, are reasonable in relation to the anticipated benefits to the subjects and in relation to the importance of knowledge that may be expected to result.

Animal Subjects

1. Animal subjects must be identified by species, strains, ages, sex, and the number of animals to be used.

2. Justify the use of animals and the choice of animals. A strong case must be made for the use of animals that are expensive or in short supply.

3. Describe veterinary care procedures.

4. Provide for and describe procedures that limit discomfort, distress, pain, and injury to an amount that is unavoidable in the conduct of scientifically sound research. However, these procedures must be designed so that they do not confound the experimental results.

5. Describe any method of euthanasia to be used and the reasons for its selection. Be sure that the method is consistent with the recommendations of the Panel on Euthanasia of the American Veterinary Medical Association. If you cannot use these methods, present a justification for using other methods.

ABSTRACT

The abstract is vitally important for the same reason the title is important. It is used as a summary for what is being proposed and how it will be done. It must, therefore, communicate the content of the proposed project succinctly and accurately, without reference to the entire application. Writing the abstract is an important task because some decisions about your application may be made only on the basis of the abstract. The impulse to dash the abstract off in the last minutes before the application goes into the mail should be resisted. A reasonable length for an abstract is about 250 words, approximately one double-spaced page. Even if the length is not specified, we recommend that this restriction be used.

The abstract should include the project's broad long-term objectives and specific aims. The importance of the project should be outlined in sufficient detail so that someone reading only the abstract can be persuaded that the project is worthy. The abstract is not the place for a complete literature review; however, sufficient information needs to be provided to place the proposed project in a scientific context. Your previous work can be referenced if it leads to the current research. However, this is not the place for a lengthy review of that research or for a discussion of the line of reasoning culminating in the current project proposal. We recommend that you describe the design and methods for achieving the project objectives. A statement of the relationship between the project and the mission of the funding source is an important component of the abstract. The importance of clarity and efficiency in stating this relationship cannot be overestimated.

LITERATURE CITED

This section is one that is often viewed as tedious and difficult because of the detail involved in each citation. It is important, however, to be as conscientious about it as about every other section. References that are incorrect or incomplete, misspelled names, omitted citations, or citations included for articles not referenced can all be viewed as indications of carelessness.

Complete citations should be used, including title, names of all authors, journal volume number, page numbers, year of publication, book publishers, place of publication, volume number, and publication year. Use your customary citation style if you wish, but be consistent. If you do not have a favorite style, we recommend the American Psychological Association (APA) style manual. Some citation styles do not include titles, therefore, these styles are not appropriate for project applications, unless application instructions state that titles be omitted. The titles of articles and books can be helpful to reviewers in their consideration of the merit of the proposed project.

The citation order is determined by the referencing system used in the text. If a numbering system is used, citations are listed in order of appearance in the text. If the author-year system is used, the citations are listed alphabetically by author. We recommend the author-year system and the APA format.

ACTION STRATEGIES

Review Project Plan for Completeness

After you have written the specific aims and hypotheses reflecting what you intend to accomplish, ask a colleague to review the procedures and other research sections for omissions. Familiarity with procedures and subject characteristics can result in a sketchy description. Keep in mind that the procedure and subject descriptions must provide enough information so that the reviewer can visualize what you plan.

We recommend that you delay having a colleague review your plan until you have a good command of it, because you undoubtedly will get suggestions for including other variables and different procedures. Listen to these suggestions and use what you can, but do not feel compelled to significantly modify your plan unless a colleague points out a fatal flaw. If this happens, go back to the drawing board.

Reread the instructions from your funding source and compare them point-by-point with what you have written in the research plan. Be particularly attentive to policies about inclusion of women and minority populations as subjects, investigators, and research personnel.

Read journal articles in areas of research involved to learn what subject information is customarily provided, what procedural details are included, and the extent of instrumentation detail. This probably is what reviewers also consider customary information. Include at least the minimum material generally found and present it in a conventional and lucid manner.

Abstract

Give the abstract as much attention as the rest of the application. Some funding sources circulate only the abstract to some of the reviewers. Therefore, the abstract is an important component of the project application. Do not overlook instructions that might be included about how the abstract should look and what should be included. See Figure 10.1 for a sample completed abstract page from the PHS 398 application packet. Note that the instructions are an integral part of the form.

Check Human and Animal Subject Policies

Contact the Institutional Review Board (IRB) or the Institutional Animal Care and Use Committee (IACUC) early so that your procedural and subject plans comply with the rules and regulations. For example, if your subjects are considered a vulnerable population, both extra time and extra procedures must be included in your application timetable and your research plan. It is a waste of time to design a project that cannot be approved by the human or animal protection committees.

Funded Grants and Funded PIs

Looking through a funded project application can give you an idea of what a completed application looks like. However, do not use an application for determining the rules of the funding source. For these rules, you must use the application materials provided, if for no other reason than that they might be quite different, even from one funding cycle to the next.

Talking with currently successful PIs can also be helpful. But again, the information you get from these conversations cannot be substituted for reading the funding source's application materials and guidelines. Also, remember that the experiences of a person whose application was being reviewed a year before your review will not necessarily be the same as yours.

BB

Principal Investigator/Program Director *(Last, first, middle):* Someone, John Z.

DESCRIPTION: State the application's broad, long-term objectives and specific aims, making reference to the health relatedness of the project. Describe concisely the research design and methods for achieving these goals. Avoid summaries of past accomplishments and the use of the first person. This abstract is meant to serve as a succinct and accurate description of the proposed work when separated from the application. **DO NOT EXCEED THE SPACE PROVIDED.**

The overall goal of this study is to develop a monitoring system and to evaluate the effectiveness of a community-based intervention designed to reduce the incidence and spread of HIV/AIDS and needle use among injecting drug abusers, their sexual partners, and individuals at demonstrated risk for injecting drug use not in treatment. The study will be conducted in a low-prevalence area by the University, in collaboration with the community council and the volunteers' association. The specific study aims are to: (1) Establish a monitoring system (N=2928); (2) Complete a formative pilot study to refine the interventions for rural and Appalachians during the initial six months; (3) Recruit 1066 injecting drug users and sex partners into two levels of the interventions; (4) Randomly assign 533 subjects recruited in the study monitoring phase to each of two levels of intervention (CDC Standard Intervention; Enhanced Intervention, developed by NIDA); (5) Conduct a process-and-outcome evaluation to assess the efficacy of the two levels of the intervention using established instrumentation; (6) Target rural and Appalachian drug abusers who will make up at least 25% (N=732) of the study monitoring system subjects and 25% (N=266) of study intervention subjects who, based on preliminary/pilot studies, are at high risk for HIV and examine risks and possible differences, including migrations; and (7) Cooperate with NIDA for standard data collection, evaluation, analyses, and publications.

PERSONNEL ENGAGED ON PROJECT, INCLUDING CONSULTANTS/COLLABORATORS. *Use continuation pages as needed* to provide the required information in the format shown below on *all* individuals participating in the scientific execution of the project.

Name J.Z. Someone	Degree(s) BS, MA, Ph.D.	Social Security No. 000-00-0000
Position Title Professor	Date of Birth (MM/DD/YY) 9/14/45	Role on Project PI
Organization University of Onestate		Department Psychiatry
Name A. Ashcroft	Degree(s) BS, MA, Ph.D.	Social Security No. 000-00-0000
Position Title Professor	Date of Birth (MM/DD/YY) 8/26/48	Role on Project Co-PI
Organization University of Onestate		Department Sociology
Name B. Bankcroft	Degree(s) BA, MS, Ph.D.	Social Security No. 000-00-0000
Position Title Professor	Date of Birth (MM/DD/YY) 7/19/47	Role on Project Statistician
Organization University of Onestate		Department Statistics
Name C. Croft	Degree(s) BS, MS, Ph.D.	Social Security No. 000-00-0000
Position Title Doctoral Fellow	Date of Birth (MM/DD/YY) 6/21/53	Role on Project Project Director
Organization University of Onestate		Department Behavioral Science
Name D. Danforth	Degree(s) BS, MS, Ph.D.	Social Security No. 000-00-0000
Position Title Professor	Date of Birth (MM/DD/YY) 6/14/51	Role on Project Consultant
Organization University of Otherstate		Department Sociology
Name	Degree(s)	Social Security No.
Position Title	Date of Birth (MM/DD/YY)	Role on Project
Organization		Department
Name	Degree(s)	Social Security No.
Position Title	Date of Birth (MM/DD/YY)	Role on Project
Organization		Department

PHS 398 (Rev. 9/91)   Page 2   BB
Number pages consecutively at the bottom throughout the application. Do *not* use suffixes such as 3a, 3b.

Figure 10.1. Sample Completed Abstract Page

REFERENCES

American Psychological Association. (1988). *Publication manual* (3rd ed.). Washington, DC: American Psychological Association.

Cooper, H. M. (1989). *Integrating research: A guide to literature reviews* (2nd ed.). Newbury Park, CA: Sage.

Kerlinger, F. N. (1964). *Foundations of behavioral research.* New York: Holt, Rinehart and Winston.

National Research Council. (1992). *Combining information: Statistical issues and opportunities for research.* Washington, DC: National Academy.

U.S. Department of Health and Human Services, Public Health Service. (1991). *Grant application form PHS 398* (p. 20). Washington, DC: U.S. Government Printing Office.

11

Supporting Details

M ost applications, in addition to requiring a project plan, require detailed information about the cost of the proposed project for all years (budget). The applications also require information about the investigators' credentials (biographical sketches), the ability of the investigators' environment to support the proposed project (resources and environment), and the extent to which the investigators have funds from other external sources (other support). Appendices may or may not be allowed. All of this information is not necessarily required with submission of the application, but is usually required before a funding decision is made.

New investigators often underestimate the importance of these sections because they appear to be forms, and at first glance, they seem to fall into a category of information that is requested and never used. However, each of these sections is associated with a specific aspect of the project and provides information about the strength of the PI's location and documentation of the ability of the PI and co-investigators to complete the proposed project. A brief discussion of the material generally included in the support documentation follows.

BUDGET AND BUDGET JUSTIFICATION

The budget materials are composed of three parts. The first part is the presentation of costs for all project components that account for the direct costs, the second is the justification for these costs, and the third is the indirect costs or overhead charged by the applicant organization.

Budget

The budget items are determined by the proposed research and the indirect cost agreement is negotiated by your organization. Budget categories generally include personnel, consultants, equipment, travel, supplies, and an "other" or miscellaneous category. In most instances, each of these categories requires a justification paragraph.

The budget should be a reasonable estimate of what the project will cost. Underestimates are as detrimental as overestimates. Across-the-board cuts have become an expected occurrence from many funding sources including the federal government. "Good research requires an adequate budget. To passively accept a large reduction of an appropriate budget is to compromise the quality of the research" (Ogden, 1991, p. 47). Different strategies have been used by PIs to avoid serious funding shortfalls. No one strategy can work for each project. PIs should be sure that all personnel and materials required to complete the project are included in the budget and that succeeding years of the budget include not only increases for inflation, but that recent cost increases also be factored into the costs. For example, health insurance might be increasing at a rate of 11%, rather than at the inflation rate of 4%. Figure 11.1 is a sample first-year budget page and Figure 11.2 is a sample entire project period budget page from the PHS 398 application.

Personnel

The personnel section includes everyone who will be working with the PI on the research project. Costs for these personnel include their salaries, proportional to time required by the research, and fringe benefits. If the project crosses fiscal years, be sure to weight the salaries and fringe benefits accordingly. The names and percent effort are also listed for personnel who donate time. The placement of personnel on the budget form depends upon the instructions. Instructions on the PHS 398 application budget page define personnel as the PI and others involved in the project from the PI's organi-

DD					Principal Investigator/Program Director *(Last, first, middle)*: Someone, John Z.			

DETAILED BUDGET FOR INITIAL BUDGET PERIOD
DIRECT COSTS ONLY

	FROM	THROUGH
	7/1/97	6/30/98

PERSONNEL *(Applicant organization only)*

NAME	ROLE ON PROJECT	TYPE APPT. *(months)*	% EFFORT ON PROJ.	INST. BASE SALARY	DOLLAR AMOUNT REQUESTED *(omit cents)*		
					SALARY REQUESTED	FRINGE BENEFITS	TOTALS
Charles Harley	Principal Investigator	12	25	70,000	17,500	3,675	21,175
Vivian Stratford	Co-PI	12	15	58,500	8,775	1,843	10,618
William Riley	Invest.	12	15	50,000	7,500	1,575	9,075
Billy Kidd	Res. Tech.	12	100	25,000	25,000	4,750	29,750
				SUBTOTALS ⟶	58,775	11,843	70,618

CONSULTANT COSTS Clyde Wilmore, Ph.D., Johns Hopkins University School of
Medicine two 3-day trips @ $750 for airfare and $500 per diem

2,500

EQUIPMENT *(itemize)*
Shock generator $1,200

1,200

SUPPLIES *(itemize by category)*
Laboratory supplies $1,000
Computer supplies $700
Questionnaires 100 @ $10 = $1,000
Shop supplies 500 subj days @ $2 = $1,000

3,700

TRAVEL
One professional meeting for P.I.   2,000

PATIENT CARE COSTS	INPATIENT	–
	OUTPATIENT	–

ALTERATIONS AND RENOVATIONS *(Itemize by category)*

OTHER EXPENSES *(Itemize by category)* Subject stipends 30 @ $20 = $600
Publications costs $500; Long distance calls $500   1,600

SUBTOTAL DIRECT COSTS FOR INITIAL BUDGET PERIOD

CONSORTIUM/CONTRACTUAL COSTS

DIRECT COSTS	$		
INDIRECT COSTS	$	TOTAL ⟶	–

TOTAL DIRECT COSTS FOR INITIAL BUDGET PERIOD *(Item 7a, Face Page)* ⟶ | $ | 81,618

PHS 398 (Rev. 9/91)   (Form Page 4) Page _____   DD
Number pages consecutively at the bottom throughout the application. Do *not* use suffixes such as 3a, 3b.

Figure 11.1. Sample First Year Budget Page

EE   Principal Investigator/Program Director *(Last, first, middle)* Someone, John Z.

BUDGET FOR ENTIRE PROPOSED PROJECT PERIOD
DIRECT COSTS ONLY

BUDGET CATEGORY TOTALS		INITIAL BUDGET PERIOD *(from page 4)*	ADDITIONAL YEARS OF SUPPORT REQUESTED			
			2nd	3rd	4th	5th
PERSONNEL: *Salary and fringe benefits* Applicant organization only		70,618	73,442	76,380		
CONSULTANT COSTS		2,500	2,500	2,500		
EQUIPMENT		1,200	–	–		
SUPPLIES		3,700	3,848	4,001		
TRAVEL		2,000	2,000	2,000		
PATIENT CARE COSTS	INPATIENT	–				
	OUTPATIENT	–				
ALTERATIONS AND RENOVATIONS		–				
OTHER EXPENSES		1,600	1,664	1,730		
SUBTOTAL DIRECT COSTS		81,618	83,454	86,611		
CONSORTIUM/ CONTRACTUAL COSTS		–	–	–		
TOTAL DIRECT COSTS		81,618	83,454	86,611		

TOTAL DIRECT COSTS FOR ENTIRE PROPOSED PROJECT PERIOD *(Item 8a)* ⟶ $251,683

JUSTIFICATION (Use continuation pages if necessary):
 From Budget for Initial Period: Describe the specific functions of the personnel, collaborators, and consultants and identify individuals with appointments that are less than full time for a specific period of the year, including VA appointments.

 For All Years: Explain and justify purchase of major equipment, unusual supplies requests, patient care costs, alterations and renovations, tuition remission, and donor/volunteer costs.

 From Budget for Entire Period: Identify with an asterisk (*) on this page and justify any significant increase or decrease in any category over the initial budget period. Describe any change in effort of personnel.

 For Competing Continuation Applications: Justify any significant increases or decreases in any category over the current level of support.

Figure 11.2. Sample Project Period Budget Page

zation only. Those on the project from other organizations appear as consultants or subcontractors.

PIs, Co-PIs, and Other Investigators. The PI's contribution of effort must be at least 20 to 25%. Other investigators' efforts must reflect their project role. Co-PIs and other investigators are included in the project only when their expertise is required for its successful conduct.

Statistician. It is imperative to include a professional statistician in the budget, either by including an investigator who qualifies as a statistical expert or by including a statistical consultant.

Research Assistant and Staff Effort. Research assistant effort is determined by the time required for data collection, entry, and analysis. Staff levels of effort are determined by the activities outlined in the procedure section. These roles can include interviewers, data entry clerks, coding clerks, transcribing clerks, programmers, or lab technicians. It is important to include adequate and qualified personnel to conduct the data collection tasks. Secretarial help, although often required on projects, is usually not considered an acceptable use of project money. If you are in an organization with no resources to fill these kinds of project needs, include a secretary in the budget and write a strong justification for it, unless including a secretary is prohibited by the indirect cost agreement of your organization.

Consultants

Consultants are experts who provide advice and other substantive assistance to the PI and others on the project on an ongoing basis. Consultant travel and per diem expenses usually are included in the budget as well as an honorarium for each year of the project.

Equipment

The rules about the cost of items in the equipment category vary with the funding source. The NIH reserves this category for equipment that costs $500 or more. In general, it is recommended that equipment costing several thousand dollars not be included within a research application. Equipment this expensive should be obtained with a separate application. Equipment items that cost less than the minimum specified by the funding source might be listed as "Supplies" or as "Other."

Travel

Travel to professional meetings by the PI and co-PI to present findings is a customary budget item. However, it is prudent to keep the cost of travel as reasonable as possible and to limit trips to one per year for the PI and co-PIs. Investigators on the project usually do not receive travel funds from the budget. For multisite projects, travel fees for co-PIs to attend annual project meetings should also be included in the budget.

Supplies

This category includes all perishable items. It is best to organize these items by categories, such as data collection supplies, computer supplies, glassware, chemicals, video film, and audiotapes. When the cost per category is $1,000 or more, we recommend itemizing costs within each category. This enables the reviewers to get a more accurate picture of the scope of your plans. If animals are involved, describe them as completely as possible (e.g., the species, the number to be used, the unit purchase cost, the unit care cost, and the number of care days).

Other or Miscellaneous

This category is for items not contained within the above budget categories. These expenses may include subject reimbursement, long-distance telephone charges, mainframe computing time, postage for mail surveys, lab charges, publication costs, page charges, books, rentals and leases, equipment maintenance, or minor fee-for-service contracts (e.g., one-time programmer fee). It is important that all of the expenses associated with the data collection be carefully tallied so that nothing is forgotten. If there is no budget item, reviewers cannot assume the work will be done.

Indirect Costs

Indirect costs are those costs that are paid to the applicant organization to support the project. Generally speaking, these costs include utilities, building and lab maintenance, secretarial support, research support personnel, graduate student support, and upkeep of libraries. Indirect cost rates have recently received scrutiny by Congress and others who have come to question excessive or unreasonable costs used to construct the indirect cost rate. Several universities have had difficulties with costs that are used as the base for their indirect costs. Indirect costs vary by organization; for universities they range from 31% to 74% with the majority being between 43% and 63%. The rates reflect differences among schools in terms of size and organization of research effort, age and condition of facilities, local costs of utilities and labor, and accounting practices. The rates are arrived at through negotiations between a federal audit agency and individual universities. The rates generally remain in effect for 2 to 3 years and then are renegotiated (Research and Graduate Studies, 1993). Although indirect costs are often overlooked as being part of the project budget, they do increase the bottom line and become part of the project costs. Some funding sources will not pay indirect costs; others state the maximum rate they will pay. The indirect costs become very important in the design of a project when the funding source places a funding cap that includes both the direct and indirect costs.

Budget Justification

Each budget item does not need to be justified, but it is a good idea to devote a justification paragraph to each of the primary budget categories, providing the level of detail required for communicating the importance of the expenditure. The following are some suggestions about how this might be done.

Personnel

Each project member's responsibilities should be described in sufficient detail to substantiate the need for the percent of effort requested. A statement that "the PI will oversee the entire project" is too general. However, a detailed description of research and administrative responsibilities is too specific. Responsibilities of each project member must be unique and complement those of other members so that the work of the entire project is covered. Whenever the type of project dictates that the project's personnel requirements and personnel costs deviate from the usual, describe the circumstances (e.g., some projects are particularly labor intensive).

Consultant Costs

Consultant costs, travel, lodging, and per diem expenses should be stated for each day whenever possible. A broad statement such as "consultant costs for two 3-day visits at $2,500" is too general.

Travel

It is preferred to show travel destinations. However, information on where national meetings will be held is not always known. Provide as much information as possible. We recommend that the budget not include travel to a national meeting to present data early in the first year of the project. However, if results will be available early in the first year, be sure that reviewers have that information.

Equipment

Explain the need for equipment purchases. Keep in mind that funding sources have a definition for equipment (e.g., equipment that costs $500 or more). In many cases, the most expensive equipment model cannot be justified, but if the most expensive model is required for the project, carefully document the need. Most often it is difficult to get equipment funded within a project grant because of the scarcity of funds. Before including equipment in a project budget, seek out other sources of equipment funding.

BIOGRAPHICAL SKETCHES

Biographical sketches are generally required for all key project personnel. Key personnel are those involved directly in the project. Biographical sketches must be written and prepared according to the instructions provided by the funding source. In general, this includes the individual's formal credentials and a list of publications. Even if a page limitation is not placed on biographical information, we recommend limiting it to two pages. Do not include an exhaustive list of recent publications but rather a selection of recent publications relevant to the proposed project. Figure 11.3 is a sample "Biographical Sketch" page from the PHS 398 application.

OTHER SUPPORT

Other support information is required for all key personnel on the project. Other support includes financial assistance for current projects in which the PI or co-investigators are involved. The information usually required by funding sources includes the project title, duration, award amount, funding

FF   Principal Investigator/Program Director *(Last, first, middle):* Someone, John Z.

BIOGRAPHICAL SKETCH

Give the following information for the key personnel and consultants and collaborators. Begin with the principal
investigator/program director. Photocopy this page for each person.

NAME	POSITION TITLE
John Z. Someone	Professor

EDUCATION *(Begin with baccalaureate or other initial professional education, such as nursing, and include postdoctoral training.)*

INSTITUTION AND LOCATION	DEGREE	YEAR CONFERRED	FIELD OF STUDY
College	B.S.	1965	Social Science
University	M.A.	1967	Behavioral Science
University	Ph.D.	1970	Behavioral Science

RESEARCH AND PROFESSIONAL EXPERIENCE: Concluding with present position, list, in chronological order, previous employment, experience, and
honors. Key personnel include the principal investigator and any other individuals who participate in the scientific development or execution of the project.
Key personnel typically will include all individuals with doctoral or other professional degrees, but in some projects will include individuals at the masters or
baccalaureate level provided they contribute in a substantive way to the scientific development or execution of the project. Include present membership on
any Federal Government public advisory committee. List, in chronological order, the titles, all authors, and complete references to all publications during the
past three years and to representative earlier publications pertinent to this application. If the list of publications in the last three years exceeds two pages,
select the most pertinent publications. DO NOT EXCEED TWO PAGES.

PROFESSIONAL EXPERIENCE:

SELECTED PUBLICATIONS:

Figure 11.3. Biographical Sketch Page

source, amount of effort committed, a brief project description, and a statement about extent of overlap within the proposed project.

RESOURCES AND ENVIRONMENT

Special care needs to be given to this section because it provides information about the ability of the PI's location to support the proposed project. The funding source may provide categories for required information. However, if categories are not provided, we suggest general information about laboratory facilities, clinical facilities and access patterns, animal care facilities, computer facilities, office space and available technology, or other special facilities that your research will rely upon.

Information about the availability of necessary equipment—together with information about location, availability, maintenance plans for vulnerable equipment, and related information—assures reviewers that a project can be completed. If your research requires major equipment and this equipment is not included in your budget, it is critical that it be mentioned in this section so reviewers are assured of its availability. Additional general information can also increase the reviewers' confidence in the ability of your location to support the project. For example, the availability of colleagues, the fall-back technology arrangements that are regularly in place, and the regular consulting resources available, such as statisticians or computer programmers, can be reviewed and discussed. The length of this section should be set by the number and extent of resources described.

PROGRAM INCOME

Some projects have the potential for generating income for the PI and his or her organization. Funding sources vary in their requirements for reporting income earned as a result of a project they funded. Regulations also often vary between profit and nonprofit recipients of funds.

The NIH defines program income as "gross income earned by a research grant recipient from activities part or all of which are borne as a direct cost by the grant" (U.S. Department of Health and Human Services, Public Health Service, 1992, p. 32), and requires that program income be reported on the "Other Support" page of the PHS 398 packet. The following are examples of program income shown in the packet:

- Fees earned from services performed under the grant, such as those resulting from laboratory drug testing
- Rental or usage fees, such as those earned from fees charged for use of computer equipment purchased with grant funds
- Third-party patient reimbursement for hospital or other medical services, such as insurance payments for patients where such reimbursement occurs because of the grant-supported activity
- Funds generated by the sale of commodities, such as tissue cultures, cell lines, or research animals
- Patent or copyright royalties

ADHERENCE TO FEDERAL REGULATIONS BY THE APPLICANT ORGANIZATION

Funding sources usually want to be assured that the applicant organization is in compliance with any regulations impinging upon the funded project. The Public Health Service requires assurances and certification, as appropriate, in the areas listed below. These also serve as a reference for other funding sources.

Human Subjects
Vertebrate Animals
Inventions and Patents
Debarment and Suspension (of PI, co-PI, and research personnel)
Drug-Free Workplace
Lobbying
Delinquent Federal Debt (This refers to the PI's organization, not to the PI)
Misconduct in Science
Civil Rights
Handicapped Individuals
Sex Discrimination
Age Discrimination

APPENDIX

When an application is submitted with the PHS 398 packet, the appendix *cannot* include material essential to the evaluation of the project. An appendix can only be used to give expanded information about something that is fully explained in the text of the proposal, because reviewers are not obligated to read the appendices. Presenting complete information in the body of the document is recommended as a regular practice, even if the funding source does not place restrictions on the appendix material. Forcing reviewers to page to the back of the document for relevant information consumes their time and energy and can influence review decisions.

ACTION STRATEGIES

Use Only Approved Application Forms

Do not use computer software to produce application forms without approval from the funding source. The extent to which the forms are permitted to deviate from provided forms varies across funding sources.

REFERENCES

Ogden, T. E. (1991). *Research proposals: A guide to success.* New York: Raven.
Research and Graduate Studies (RGS). (1993). *Research and Graduate Studies Newsletter.* Lexington: University of Kentucky.
U.S. Department of Health and Human Services, Public Health Service. (1991). *Grant application form PHS 398* (p. 32). Washington, DC: U.S. Government Printing Office.

12

Work Plan

Some of us have probably had occasion to notice that there are people who travel and people who get someplace. Developing a written plan, however brief, for achieving a goal increases the odds of achieving that goal. Devising a work plan or timetable is invaluable for orientation during a complex project, whether it be long-term or for a relatively short timeframe. A timetable can guide you when you don't want to waste time or when you need to be engaged in additional projects. It also enables more efficient distribution of activities when you must rely on the availability of others. A timetable makes it clear when you need to apply pressure or when you can use gentle persuasion tactics to get agreed-upon work done on time. This chapter briefly discusses timetable development and use in general and then provides sample timetables for project development and for application development that can be customized by investigators to meet their particular needs.

A timetable provides an outline of what you wish to accomplish and includes the time restrictions imposed by other commitments, by those with whom you wish to work, by organizational requirements of your home site and your collaborators, by the funding source, and by your level of energy. The available energy for intellectual work is often not factored into work plans because we use a calendar in a straightforward way; if there is a blank time and someone has a request, we pencil it in. The fact is, you can plan to write several pages for the application from 1 p.m. to 3 p.m. on Monday, Wednesday, and Friday, but if you spend the remaining time in stressful meetings, devising other research procedures, or struggling with a data analysis program, it will be difficult to complete the planned writing.

A work plan for a project begins with a review of how you regularly distribute your work effort, including the end products such as giving a lecture or mailing an article to be reviewed for publication. One way to begin constructing a work plan is simply to list the percentage of time spent on primary work categories. For example, you might allot 25% effort for teaching, 15% effort for research, 35% effort for patient care, 3% effort for administration, and the remaining 22% effort for service activities. In this hypothetical distribution of effort, successful development of a research project is not possible; the remaining 15% effort is just not enough time.

REASONS FOR DEVELOPING AND USING A TIMETABLE

Reasons for developing and using a timetable vary from one individual to the next. The following are a few reasons for developing a timetable that influence a project's development.

Allow Time to Test Fledgling Ideas

Developing a work plan as soon as you experience enthusiasm for a project is a good way to concentrate your thoughts and assess the effort required by the project. This work plan—the display of your current daily, weekly, and monthly activities—reveals the amount of time you have to spend on the new project without changing your current schedule. If the time available for the project is before 7 a.m., after 9 p.m., or on your lunch hour, it is our opinion that you do not have adequate time to assess the feasibility of a project nor develop an application. A work plan will help you and others decide on how your distribution of effort can be rearranged to position project time so that you will have intellectual energy to do the required thinking, planning, meeting, and writing.

Matching the Project Calendar Against the Social Calendar

Less time is available for project development in some seasons of the year than others. Deadlines early in the year are the most difficult to meet because of the late fall and winter holidays. However, other times of year also have holidays as well as unexpected natural events such as floods, tornadoes, hurricanes, and earthquakes that can interfere with both project production and mailing. The project timetable must take into account all regular occurring events that will take away from project time, whether they be national or specific to your organization (e.g., end of term papers to read and grades to submit). The only safeguard against unexpected delays (e.g., breakdown of express mail vehicles or breakdown of copy machines) is to plan submitting the application before the last possible day.

Establishing Priorities

A decision to submit an application must temporarily change your career goals and, therefore, the distribution of your work effort across categories.

A distribution of effort that requires 25% effort for teaching, 15% effort for research, 35% effort for patient care, 3% effort for administration, and the remaining 22% effort for service activities reflects your organization's time priorities and perhaps reflected your priorities before you decided to submit a project application. An application probably will not be completed if you cannot cut back on service effort or jettison a prior goal, say, of increasing the number of weekly activities, thereby boosting the 35% effort to 45%. A new goal, accompanied by additional work and responsibilities, cannot be achieved by using the old work plan. The new goal must be reflected in your percentage of effort in each category and in the work plan within these categories. Keep in mind that although display by day or week appears to be a more detailed plan of work, it is merely a chronological ordering of the activities that might occur within a particular period. This chronological display is a useful display of your current schedule and can be used to assess the feasibility of adding the activities of the new project.

Most people organize activities by time of day. Do not mistake the time-of-day ordering for a priority ordering. A new investigator's priorities must be the engine that runs his or her daily activities. For this reason, it is critical for a new investigator to take control of her or his daily calendar. It is a mistake to think that schedules can continue to be done as they have been done in the past and have the result promote the activities involved in your new goal. Keep in mind that time is used not only for tangible product development but also for the intangible process—thinking. The latter activity, because it does not have an immediate tangible outcome, is routinely absent from work plans, especially when someone other than the new investigator has control of the daily calendar.

Energy Level

A personal level of energy and motivation for both creative and tedious work are variables with a considerable influence on an application's quality. On some days, more energy is available for creativity, and on some days more is available for tedious work. In practical terms, this means that priorities will change from day-to-day. A timetable is essentially a list of these different kinds of work and provides a way to choose that which you are able to do. Using a timetable to direct your energy most efficiently enables you to maintain forward movement of the project. Each day you know that some progress is being made toward your expressed goal.

Procrastination and Timetables

Can a work plan or timetable help procrastinators? The answer to the question is yes and no, depending upon the kinds of procrastination under discussion. Most people engage in procrastination at one time or another. Sometimes, even though it is called procrastination, an activity is delayed because of an uneasiness about the level of available information. In this instance, whatever it is called, delaying until a satisfactory level of information is available is constructive. If you believe you routinely put off doing things, analyze your behavior to see whether you put off doing some things but not others. Your choices of activities might provide a clue for developing a strategy to complete the application within the prescribed timeframe.

SETTING THE PROJECT AND APPLICATION CLOCKS

The temporal tension created by the decision to complete a project application is related to allotting enough time to prepare a competitive application but not so much time as to produce apathy during the final days.

As with any writing task, completing the application becomes tedious. However, unlike many other writing tasks, the stakes remain high to the end. It is helpful to set the application clock ticking with two clocks in tandem: The first clock starts ticking when the project first intrigues you; the second clock, when you begin preparing the application.

EXAMINING AN IDEA: TIMEFRAME SUGGESTIONS

Ideas about potential studies and projects are common for investigators. The experienced investigator and the new investigator alike are sometimes wary of these ideas at first (engagement of the first clock). The incubation time for ideas and the timeframe for confidence that the idea is both researchable and fundable vary for individuals. But in general, we find that arriving at a conclusion about these rarely requires less than 6 to 12 months or no more than 2 years. Procrastination, rather than difficulties with the idea, might be driving deliberation that extends beyond two years. With the variability among investigators, we cannot suggest a standard timetable but only general guidelines for those activities involved in developing an idea to the point where application preparation begins (engagement of the second clock).

Preliminary Decision About a Research Topic

It is usual after the first excitement of an idea has passed for investigators to notice that the scope of the project is too broad, that the procedures required would never be approved by an Institutional Review Board, that the subjects desired are not available in the numbers required, that additional expertise is required, or that any number of concerns impinging on the project require adjustments of some kind. These are not daunting discoveries, because everyone engaged in project development has had some practice in resolving these issues. At this developmental stage of the project, these kinds of issues need to be resolved with information while the new investigator retains the decision process. That is, you don't want to intentionally or unintentionally acquire co-investigators. The reasoning for this is that resolving these issues often modifies the original project idea. Sometimes the modified idea is not even a recognizable relative of the original. At other times, the modification shifts the focus to require including another scientific discipline, a new methodology, or consultants that would not have been a part of the original project. Thus the modified project idea must undergo careful scrutiny, and again the most basic questions must be answered regarding its importance, usefulness, timetables, and doability. The new resolution may suggest a pilot study to strengthen the argument. Keep in mind, however, that the pilot study must focus on answering pertinent questions. If the research includes hypotheses that require a scientific discipline in addition to yours or research methodology outside of your expertise, gather as much information as you can through seminars, conversations, and research articles to assess the feasibility of your plan. With this background, you will be able to profitably discuss pertinent issues with others who have the needed expertise.

Our suggestion that you do this preliminary work by yourself with informal conversations does not mean that you should refrain from discussing your idea with other investigators. It probably is beneficial to run ideas by others as opportunities arise, during seminars, hallway conversations, or national meetings. The point we want to make is that you should not yoke yourself to a particular colleague as a potential co-investigator until you have explicitly decided what you want to do. This decision includes the theory or theories to support your ideas and the overall procedures you think adequate for collecting data. This process, in our experience, takes at least 6 months.

Literature Review and Meetings

Although time consuming, a careful and complete reading of the pertinent literature is imperative because this knowledge will enable you to write a comprehensive literature review while citing only the literature directly relevant to your topic. You might already have published an article with a review of the literature, or you may have to start from scratch. If the latter is the case, it is best to allow at least 2 months to gather the material and integrate it with your topic. If you have published an article using a review of the pertinent literature, guard against being nonchalant in your assessment of its comprehensiveness and relevance to the new project. Even though the reviews have come from research within the same area, a new project, by definition, covers new ground. Consider the literature pertaining to the new hypotheses, and consider updating the review. To neglect updating an existing literature review is to risk investing time in planning research that has already been done.

Many advantages can be gained from moving through this first phase slowly. In our opinion, you need time to scrutinize and reflect on all aspects of the current literature and your ideas in light of that literature. Do not attempt to measure your productivity during this period by the number of pages written. Because writing is thinking on paper, you will probably be doing some writing. In fact, we believe writing improves clarity of thought. During this phase, however, emphasis should be on thinking, not on producing drafts. Problems and research issues occur in layers. More often than not, solving one dilemma or settling on one strategy reveals another layer of issues. Allowing time to mull over the implications of tentative solutions produces a solid rationale and a project plan that are more likely to withstand the scrutiny of your colleagues and a funding source review group.

After you have shaped the hypotheses and written a solid literature review, it is time to meet with colleagues and knowledgeable research personnel to critique your plan. Whether these meetings are one-on-one or in a group depends upon your style and the issues. Some investigators prefer to meet with those whom they want to recruit. Others choose colleagues who are knowledgeable but who may not be a part of the project. Either strategy will provide the needed information, especially if a carefully thought-out plan is presented. During these sessions you will present the research rationale, procedures, design, and outcome measures. The aim of this meeting is to uncover the strengths and weaknesses of your plan and provide suggestions about filling in gaps or moving the project to a different level. Keep in mind that the depth of critique is related to your plan's level of excellence. Unfortunately, even though you have now been thinking about this project for several months and believe that every *t* has been crossed and every *i* dotted, there is still the possibility that the plan can benefit from additional modification to data collection procedures, subject recruitment procedures, or data collection instruments. Meetings of this kind also place investigators in a position to assess the need for and recruit co-investigators.

After recruiting co-investigators and research staff, meetings to more finely hone the project should be planned with them to keep everyone fully informed about the project's development. These meetings usually produce additional opinions about the project, greater depth and breadth in the literature review, and assurance of the feasibility of project components under the purview of the other investigator(s). The investigator's style also influences how these meetings are conducted. Some investigators prefer to have some one-on-one meetings with the potential co-investigator(s) to iron out misconceptions or disagreements in private. Then after the research plan has reached a higher level of refinement, opinions from co-investigators, consultants, and advisers are sought at meetings where particular attention is paid to the importance, doability, and timeliness of the project, as well as to entertaining questions about whether the cost of the project as finally designed is worth the outcome. Other investigators prefer to have these meetings with co-investigators, consultants, and advisers early in the project development period.

We recommend that you develop a meeting timetable to present to the project group. Distribute the timetable at your first meeting and ask for suggestions on its modification. This timetable will depend upon how often it is realistic to hold meetings (some investigators may have to travel), how many meetings are required, and the mandatory participants (perhaps not everyone needs to attend each time). We suggest that no more than four 1-hour meetings be scheduled. Busy investigators have an interest in maximizing efficiency and appreciate a concerted effort to make each meeting valuable. If at the conclusion of the fourth meeting there is a clear need for and an interest in having additional meetings, schedule them. We recommend that a maximum of 2 months be planned for these meetings.

Face-to-face meetings are important during the early phases of the project. However, after the group has become acquainted, telephone calls and electronic mail can be effective means of communication. In fact, we recommend that electronic mail become as common a communication tool as the telephone or FAX. We suggest, however, that e-mail and FAX should not be used until you are fairly well-acquainted with the group to obviate the chance of misunderstandings. An additional factor to consider when using e-mail and FAX is that of confidentiality. Neither of these methods provide the privacy of telephone conversations or regular mail, with e-mail being the most public. Organize your thoughts before each communication and use the telephone when necessary, but keep in mind that unplanned telephone calls can interrupt the person you are calling. Let your colleagues know that you value their time and understand that they have other priorities.

Although we continually stress the importance of doing work at a high level of quality, this does not mean that perfection is a goal. Throughout this process, be prepared to accept limitations in knowledge, resources, or intelligence. Only rarely is the ideal research project planned and implemented under ideal circumstances.

Table 12.1   Preapplication Tasks

Month	Topic
0	First idea about a project
1	Meeting with supervisor to assess schedule changes to accommodate developing the idea
2	Decision about research idea
3	Reappraisal of idea
4-5	Informal discussions with colleagues
6	Assessment of the availability of subjects
	Assessment of the ability of your location to support the research
7-8	Literature review
9-10	Discussions with investigators in your area of expertise and other disciplines about procedures, literature, and data collection methods
11-12	Pilot study (only as extensive as needed to gather information)
13	Meetings with investigators with intention of recruiting them as co-investigators on your project
14-15	Meetings with investigators and research personnel to discuss and refine the project
16	Assessing project cost relative to value of outcomes
17	Penultimate decisions on all aspects of research project and final decisions on the composition of the research group
18	Decision to locate a funding source and review its requirements and application receipt dates

Application Submission Decision

Only after the literature review and the co-investigator meetings are complete is it useful to discuss a submission deadline. In view of the work required to determine whether an idea can be translated into a project application, setting a submission deadline before completion of that process can be frustrating and can produce co-investigator disenchantment. When the research topic is sufficiently defined, the scope of the project clarified, and the outcomes agreed upon, identifying a funding source and determining its deadline and reviewing application information are possible.

A timetable of the events to be completed before making a submission decision would include, but not be restricted to, the items in Table 12.1. Table 12.1 provides suggested times, but the times allowed for each item are clearly idiosyncratic.

COMPLETING THE APPLICATION: TIMEFRAME SUGGESTIONS

A review of the funding source criteria, especially receipt deadlines, will inform the PI's decision about the time needed to complete the application. We assume that a new investigator who has never submitted an application will need from 6 to 9 months to complete the application materials, keeping in mind that an application with no co-investigators will require less time than one with several co-investigators. Completing a project application is a substantial undertaking that requires the investigator to play a variety of roles over a considerable time. A timetable of the events culminating in mailing a competitive application clarifies the size and complexity of the overall task.

A project plan is usually longer than a journal article and is developed to persuade, not to report. The project application has additional components that substantiate your ability to complete the project and your organization's willingness and ability to support your effort. The way to move comfortably through a complex project like an application is to set up an orderly progression of intermediate goals and subgoals. This strategy enables sustained energy and enthusiasm throughout the course of the project because each subgoal has its foundation in the previous day's work. A proposal is written much in the same way as Mt. Everest is climbed—one step at a time, with each step the preparation for the next. The minimum time required to complete an application is about 3 months. If your project involves an area in which you need to review literature and examine alternate methodologies, allow 12 months. However, do not allow a timetable to extend beyond 12 months.

The timetable incorporates all application components and activities associated with their completion. This representation clarifies the distribution of the intermediate and subgoals to achieve the final goal of a completed application. A timetable gives daily direction to your efforts, guides the concerns you should attend to, and most importantly provides small units to work with, lightening the entire psychological effort. With a written timetable, all you need to keep in mind is the immediate task. If each task is completed each day, the application will be completed. Therefore, there need be no concerns about finishing the application on time. The energy usually expended on such concerns can be more fruitfully used on resolving project issues. Timetables are most useful when not viewed as being written in stone. Before an application is finished, many investigators construct several timetables. Each successive timetable includes additional details that become apparent only as the project progresses.

Another feature of a timetable is its ability to sharpen the immediacy of future deadlines. Two primary goals are associated with developing an application. The first primary goal is to decide, on the basis of the preliminary assessment information, to write an application and organize the associated work. The deadline date for this decision is determined in part by the funding source's deadline, the extent of pilot work, and the ease of establishing a work group. The second primary goal is to submit a competitive application. This deadline, however, could be 12 months or even only 12 weeks in the future. Deadlines that are not immediate often take on an aura of unreality, and for some even a deadline as near as 12 weeks is not real. The belief is that when the time comes the necessary tasks will either be completed or be quickly accomplished. Sometimes this is the case; at other times the tasks are completed but at the sacrifice of quality; and sometimes deadlines are just not met. A few days, in most instances, is not enough time to develop a competitive application. Whether you work best with immediate deadlines or prefer to complete work early, organizing work by assigning deadlines to intermediate goals and subgoals accommodates both work styles. These intervening goals are organized by completion dates. This type of timetable is most easily constructed in reverse order. That is, the first date is the funding source receipt date, and the second date is the date you plan to mail the proposal. Planning your effort over the time available, in reverse order, forces the later and more rigid bureaucratic deadlines to be taken into account first. It should be noted that it is not uncommon for bureaucratic requirements to consume at the very least the 2-week period before the mailing date.

Intermediate Goals and Subgoals

Before a timetable can be developed, a new investigator needs a list of the project's intermediate goals and subgoals. Intermediate goals are those things that must be done if the application is to be competitive. The subgoals are additional tasks and activities promoting completion of an intermediate goal. Table 12.2 presents a sample list of intermediate goals beginning with the funding source receipt date and followed by a primary goal of mailing a competitive application. In a timetable, each item and each additional subgoal is associated with a date. Work style determines the time lapse between items. For example, first drafts might be written very quickly, but more time is required for second drafts. This should be reflected in your timetable. If you are still doing a good deal of the thinking and planning while writing the first draft, only compressed time remains for the second draft. In this case, plan to delegate some of the second draft work to a colleague, a co-investigator, or a secretary to keep your work within the prescribed timeframe. If a co-investigator will write a section, include in your timetable the expected start day for the work, intervals at which you will contact the writer to assess progress and offer assistance, and the final date you must receive the section. In a similar vein, if you know that a co-investigator might procrastinate about sending you information, allow for several reminders spaced at reasonable intervals. Do not give the supporting documents short shrift. If you expect to get poorly copied or out-of-date support material, allow time for your secretarial staff to produce documents of the required quality.

A timetable should be designed to meet your personal work style and pace and to allow interdigitation with your co-investigators. When preparing an application, do not frustrate yourself by trying to change to someone else's work style and pace, and don't try to change someone else's work style and pace either. Remember, this is not the time to develop new work habits! Design a timetable that accommodates work habits and has high potential for meeting the funding source deadline with a competitive application.

There is a definite timeframe within which to complete all the application tasks. This timeframe is the number of weeks from the date you begin the timetable to the funding source receipt date. That is why we recommend starting development of your timetable with the funding source receipt date. This date cannot be changed, nor can other bureaucratic procedures involved in getting an application through an organizational system. Whether you view bureaucratic procedures as barriers or opportunities to receive institutional support, they cannot be ignored and must be shown on a timetable.

Develop your list of intermediate goals and subgoals using those in Table 12.2 or an application's table of contents and assign a timeframe, in either weeks or days, to each. Figure 12.1 shows the "Table of Contents" page from the PHS 398 application.

Depending upon organizational procedures, final signatures might require 2 weeks or less, or if your organization requires a complete preproposal review, perhaps as much as 8 weeks. Our advice is to assume that not

CC   Principal Investigator/Program Director *(Last, first, middle)*: _____
Type the name of the principal investigator/program director at the top of each printed page and each continuation page. (For type specifications, **see Specific Instructions** on page 10.)

RESEARCH GRANT
TABLE OF CONTENTS

Appendix *(Five collated sets. No page numbering necessary for Appendix)*
       Number of publications and manuscripts accepted or submitted for publication *(Not to exceed 10)* _____
       Other items (list):

                                                                         ☐ Check If Appendix
                                                                              is Included

Figure 12.1. Table of Contents Page

everyone will be available on the day you want their signature. Therefore, you should give yourself some slack time around this item. The time required to assemble the final completed copy of the application is also generally underestimated. We like to allow at least 1 day for this assembly because it is better to overestimate the time needed. Be prepared for surprises during this time, such as the unexpected absence of the secretary who knows all about the project, or the most reliable copy machine breaking down, or citywide power failure.

The remaining items listed in Table 12.2 also need to be assigned timeframes. Note that Table 12.2 allows time for two drafts. This is the absolute minimum number of drafts. It is our experience that this minimum number of drafts is fine for investigators who already have great depth and breadth of experience in writing project plans. If there is enough time for an incubation period after the second draft, a third draft is often very profitable and in most instances will result in a substantially improved application. Use your past experiences with your own work, your colleagues, and your office staff to estimate the time each item requires. If you come to the end of the list and you have used more days than available, go back and make adjustments. Keep in mind that this is an estimate of time consumption, and you will be adjusting the time for each item as the application is developed. However, when re-estimates still result in more time being needed than available, it is advisable to select a later submission date.

In Table 12.2, time periods are allotted in days and receipt dates are based upon approximately a 4-month funding source cycle, leaving four 5-day work weeks or a total of 80 days for application completion.

Assigning a timeframe within which each item is to be completed forces close scrutiny of each task and assessment of how difficult the task will be to complete in spite of minor problems. For example, the discovery that you have about 4 weeks to complete the first draft of the design section and assemble it with your specific aims and literature review in an efficient and persuasive manner will precipitate a different reaction if you are engaging in research with extensive pilot work or if you are applying methods new to you and for which you have engaged a collaborator. In the latter instance, a subgoal of meeting with the collaborator 2 weeks before you plan to have sections assembled would be a prudent action. Your timetable, therefore, should highlight the possibility of small problems that can be overcome relatively quickly with little change in overall plans and also allow provision of time for larger problems that may require the help of others and also significantly change some part of the project.

Table 12.2   Worksheet for Timetable Items

# of Days	Topic
0	Funding source receives application
1	Application mailed to funding source
1	Review by university or agency research support offices before mailing
1	Level Two signatures (university, agency. . . .)
1	Level One signatures (department, unit. . . .)
1	Assembling one complete final copy of the application
1	Matching table of contents or funding source guidelines to application
1	Assembling a final draft of the application
1	Complete budget and budget justification on forms
1	Develop budget and budget justification
1	Supporting documents*
	Check that material has been received from all investigators and that it is complete and neat
2	Complete human or animal subject protection forms
1	Check list of literature cited for accuracy and completeness
2	Write abstract
1	Review proposal critiques from other research applications
4	Review of project component by a colleague for content and logic
1	Send reminders to investigators for materials not yet received
3	Institutional Review Board application (human and animal subjects protection) are obtained and started
2	Check all components of the research plan for accuracy and completeness
5	Write second draft of the specific aims
5	Write second draft of the literature review
5	Write second draft of the research design and methods
10	Write first draft of the specific aims
10	Write first draft of the literature review
10	Write first draft of the research design and methods
2	Request supporting documents* from investigators
1	Determine administrative deadlines for your and your co-investigator's organizations
7	Request material from funding source
	Learn funding source receipt or postmark dates

* Other support, resources, and environment pages; letters of agreement and commitment; biographical information (vitae) including Social Security numbers; and other research support information.

The order of these tasks is based upon our experiences with PIs working to get an application completed. Often the supporting documents present the most difficult barriers. Therefore, we recommend that you begin early to gather supporting document information so that this phase of the project is completed by the deadline date. You might want to expand the timetable to include the names of the individuals from whom you will seek information and use the timetable as a checklist for recording receipt of the information. Table 12.2 is an example that must be modified to meet your situation and work style. We recommend that the units of work listed be kept to a reasonable size. That is why we have separated the research plan into its primary parts. If your project includes more than one scientific discipline, you might need to subdivide the literature review so that you can stay posted on how your co-investigator is doing.

It is highly recommended that a new investigator request a colleague to review the entire project plan before submitting the application. This review, which ideally should occur several weeks before the mailing deadline, puts additional time stress on the project. However, a colleague can be more helpful if asked in advance, given more than a few hours, and allowed time to recommend incorporating changes into the final document when appropriate.

Some parts of the timetable will be more difficult than others to complete. You will be able to imagine your goal clearly, but the route in terms of time consumption will not always be clear, nor will you always know every person and technique you might need to include—so make some guesses, understanding that guesses are what they are. Change the timetable if some parts move along more quickly than expected. If significant changes are required in the project, modify the timetable to accommodate time requirements, keeping in mind those unrelenting bureaucratic deadlines. Remember, Herculean effort is not to be used unless it cannot possibly be avoided, and this level of effort is certainly to be avoided if the final deadline is going to be missed. Thus the timetable plots a course that represents efficient use of your time and resources and permits restructuring as needed.

HOW TO USE A TIMETABLE

A timetable is a great way to communicate to co-investigators and everyone associated with the application the importance of keeping the project moving each day. It also clarifies the need for your associates to communicate with you about any unavoidable delays encountered. For example, if you have allotted 4 days, from November 19 to November 22, to compile the project budget, you absolutely must have it completed no later than November 26. If the person doing the budget is going to be on a Thanksgiving holiday, it would be best to know that in the early planning phases. A good way to obtain this information is to give this person a copy of your timetable, pointing out the periods when you need his or her assistance. Another example is signatures. Giving a copy of your timetable to the department chairperson or agency director will alert these people to the need for them to take action at a specific time. If they are going to be away, you can arrange to get their signatures early or learn who can sign for them, because getting a signature late is never an option, and not getting it at all is very risky.

Timetables can only help the new investigator to complete work according to schedule if they are used. The slack time built into a work plan is one aspect that makes timetables easier to use. Many tasks require more time than imagined, but because the actual time is not predictable, planned slack time allows for the needed time as well as the opportunity to stockpile time. Timetables can also be modified in the face of unexpected external events in our lives or the lives of our co-investigators. Timetables also provide opportunities for discerning what work can be done each day without fail. If you cannot overcome inertia to write the first draft of the literature review, a glance through the timetable will alert you to other tasks that need to be done, some of them by others. So you can choose a task you can do, or you can "delegate" a task, and thereby move the project forward, keeping the completion date within the timeframe you have planned.

Table 12.3 is the timetable for the items and timeframes from Table 12.2. This timetable begins with the current time and ends with the final goal of mailing the application. On the basis of the number of days required for the items, dates can now be assigned. The final date should be the funding source receipt or postmark date.

If it is possible to begin the application development earlier than expected, additional time can be allotted for items you think will require more time in view of your work habits and the volume of work required. It is a good idea to include extra time whenever possible, providing it does not slow down the project development pace.

ACTION STRATEGIES

Surviving the Ride

Accept the fact that your first foray into following work plans and timetables is going to result in some buffeting by other schedules. Even the seasoned timetable follower experiences this situation until enough information is obtained to define obstacles or patterns of interference. With this information in hand, and with practice, it is possible to develop strategies to negotiate

Table 12.3   Sample Timetable Covering a Period of 4 Months

Receipt date: June 3, 1996	
2/12-2/19	Determine funding source receipt date or postmark date
2/20	Determine bureaucratic deadlines for your organization
2/21-2/22	Request supporting documents* from investigators
2/23-3/07	First draft of research design and methods
3/08-3/21	First draft of literature review
3/22-4/04	First draft of specific aims
4/05-4/11	Second draft of research design and methods
4/12-4/18	Second draft of literature review
4/19-4/25	Second draft of specific aims
4/26-4/29	All research component sections complete
4/30-5/02	Institutional Review Board application (human and animal subjects protection)
5/03	Reminders to investigators for materials not yet received
5/06-5/09	Review of research component by a colleague for content and logic
5/10	Review of proposal critiques from other research applications
5/13-5/14	Abstract written
5/15	Literature cited accurate and complete
5/16-15/17	Human investigation forms completed
5/20	Supporting documents* collected and complete
5/21	Develop budget and budget justification
5/22	Complete budget and budget justification
5/23	Assemble a final draft of the application
5/24	Match table of contents or funding source guidelines to application
5/27	Assemble one complete final copy of the application
5/28	Level One signatures (department, unit. . . .)
5/29	Level Two signatures (agency, university. . . .)
5/30	Review by university or agency research support offices before mailing
5/31	Mail proposal to funding source
6/03	Funding source receipt or postmark date

* Other support, resources, and environment pages; letters of agreement and commitment; biographical information (vitae) including Social Security numbers; and other research support information.

obstacles and minimize the effects of interference patterns. But do not abandon your work plan or timetable! It is the mechanism that holds your attention to the required tasks. It will obviate your drifting off course into easier but only tangentially related activities.

Meetings

Prepare for meetings. Use handouts that are informative and look good. Listen carefully to questions and give answers that encourage interchange with your colleagues. Remember that questions may not always be what they seem when cross-disciplinary investigators collaborate. When necessary, take time to have explanations, concepts, or ideas presented fully. The more comfortable the group is with the project ideas, the better the final project will be.

Daily Schedule

Assign blocks of time in your daily calendar for others to fill for you, but keep control of scheduling the remaining blocks of time. Start with broad categories for determining your current distribution of effort, such as teaching, patient care, administration, and service. Preparing a work plan for your current schedule can be useful. Given your work style and the type of project planned, assess the amount of time needed and the optimal time of day.

Meet with your supervisor early in the process so she or he is not surprised when it is imperative that you claim project time. Stand firm and do not relinquish your project time. Thus you will have to say "no" to people who are not aware of your new commitments. It will not help to relent because "they didn't know and I felt I should help out." Once this pattern begins, it will not end.

Procrastinators

The literature to help procrastinators suggests that the easiest things should not be done first: Do what is hard first and get it behind you. It is our experience that project applications have enough easy things that absolutely must be done, so sometimes an easy task can be chosen over a hard one. Another thing to keep in mind is that some things appear hard because the required thinking, draft writing, or discussions have not been done. In short, the information level is not sufficient to commit to writing the foundation from which rewrites will bound.

Follow Your Timetable

Your timetable is a guide for activities related to submitting a competitive application by the date selected. The timetable, therefore, is your aid, not your master. Use it, don't fight it. The first time you develop a timetable you will allow too little time for many of the tasks. Perceive this not as a shortcoming, but rather as constructive feedback. You can adjust the timetable and retain the original application date. As you work with the application and project plan, the timetable, and your overall work schedule and work style, your timetable will more closely approximate reality.

RELATED READING

Clark, J., & Clark, S. (1992). *Prioritize Organize: The art of getting it done.* Shawnee Mission, KS: National Press Publications.

PART V

How to Write

Unique Moves

13

Writing to Be Competitive

This chapter is about writing a well-organized and persuasive grant application. It presents strategies that can enhance the clarity of the project plan and evoke thought in the reviewer. Because the reviewer has only the application from which to glean answers to questions, an application must communicate the project plans and the rationale for those plans in a clear and concise manner and be persuasive about the importance of the project. Your goal is to evoke in the reviewer the same intellectual excitement and urgency that the project evokes in you.

Previous chapters have also dealt with communication—communication with collaborators, administrative officials and staff, and funding personnel. The critical element of these communication situations, both written and oral, is successful interaction, and we have already discussed how this might be achieved. During all phases of application development, there are opportunities to either read the material or follow a conversation with a written document. In these instances, opportunities are available to go back for clarification of certain points, to get feedback, and to correct impressions when they are incorrect. There are also opportunities to receive information about thinking precision and the viability of the project designs. Previous chapters have also discussed what to include in your application that could be amplified with a telephone conversation, FAX, or e-mail.

The final application stands alone without opportunities for clarification by telephone, FAX, or e-mail. Reviewers can only review what is presented. Further explanations, expansions, or definitions are not possible. Reviewers assume that the written descriptions of the rationale, the project plan, and the plans for using the data are congruent with the PI's thoughts, conclusions, and plans. What this means is that reviewers are not likely to say, "This is what is written here, but I'll bet what is really meant is. . . . , otherwise it just won't work. . . ." It also means that your words are like spotlights that light up reviewers' information about your topic area. Reviewers use this information to understand your thoughts and draw conclusions—the best conclusions they can draw—on the basis of the information you provide.

For instance, if the intent of an application is to have the reviewers think of a "square," several critical pieces of information must be provided (e.g., the angle of the corners, the relative length of the sides, and the shape that the lines form). But if information is omitted about the length of the sides, the reviewers might assume that the sides are equal and call it a square, or they might conclude that opposite sides are equal but adjacent sides are unequal and call it a rectangle. If the reviewers make the correct choice, no harm has been done by incomplete information. However, if the reviewers make the incorrect choice, much of the remaining information could be unintelligible because the reviewers are starting with an incorrect information base. Our example is simple, but with a little thought you can notice many more variables that have not been discussed and could have an important bearing on the reviewers' conclusions. The purpose of this simple example is to emphasize the difficulty of achieving 100% fidelity when using words to transmit thoughts. It is important, however, to keep trying! The text of a project plan must provide sufficient and appropriate information to aid the reviewers to approximate a mental construction of your project as you actually will do it. An investigator's goal is to achieve this with sufficient clarity, leaving no uncertainty in the reviewers' minds.

Each reviewer reads an application differently, just as we all read a research article in our own way. The reviewer, just like you, makes judgments about what material is presented, how material is presented, and what material is left out. As much as we desire to be unfailingly objective about reported research, we often do not achieve this goal because the author fails to meet our expectations and we become frustrated at not being able to quickly comprehend designs, relevance of statistics, and reasonableness of conclusions, to name a few issues. What you need to do is what Price (1981, p. 67) suggests writers do for any reader: "[D]o not ask him to understand everything at once . . . give him a way to organize many different facts . . . let him feel forward movement."

Application reviewers, although striving for objectivity, are just like you—vulnerable to influence from the frustrations and failed expectations described above as well as the conditions under which they conduct their review. Investigators, because they want reviewers to be energized and enthusiastic about their project plans, must make their projects readily understood. This means presenting the plan so that it does not entail the level of work required for understanding a journal article. The investigator carries the burden of giving effective, persuasive, and efficient communication that enables reviewers to understand and appreciate the significance of the proposed project. It is the task of the investigator to write in a style that permits the reviewer to focus on the project rather than succumb to distraction and confusion prompted by complicated sentences and paragraphs. The investigator's goal is to keep the reviewers' heads nodding up and down. It is to be hoped that the document will produce few furrowed brows and few "Nos." Remember, the application is the only information that the reviewers have about your project. It is in your best interest, therefore, to make it as easy to read and follow as possible. The rest of the chapter presents some suggestions of how this might be done.

PHYSICAL APPEARANCE

Some reviewers quickly page through the project plan before beginning a serious review. This is done to determine how difficult it is to read and follow. In our opinion, an easily read project plan is one with the following elements:

- double spacing between paragraphs
- main sections headed and arranged as described in the funding source's application instructions
- paragraph headings and main section headings

- paragraph headings designed to provide information about the placement of the topic within the overall document. (This information can be provided by heading position, shading, or underlining. Note that the scheme must be consistent throughout the project plan.)
- paragraphs of moderate length
- moderate to short sentences with minimal use of semicolons

ORGANIZATIONAL PLAN

A well-organized project plan allows the reviewer to easily find answers to questions of intellectual curiosity such as "I wonder how this is handled?" or "What was included. . . . ?" A plan in which answers are easy to find basks in a brighter light than the one in which questions can be answered only by reading large sections or the entire narrative. Easy access to materials is promoted by carefully organizing and judiciously highlighting meaningful section and paragraph headings.

The first level of organization must be that required by the funding source. For example, the organization of the PHS 398 packet begins with Specific Aims, followed by Background and Significance, Preliminary Studies, and Research Methods and Design. The organization of information within each of these sections should follow the same pattern whenever possible. It is our opinion that the order should be arranged to engage the thought processes of the reviewer, enabling him or her to understand the validity of the arguments presented. It must be assumed that this train of thought is novel to the reviewer. Because of this, care must be taken to include all relevant pieces of information, excluding information not integral to your arguments. The order and quality of information must be such that prior conclusions about the literature's implications, embedded in the reviewer's frame of reference, do not intrude. If there is no content-driven order, present the most exciting or most productive aspects first.

The Specific Aims section establishes the information pattern for the associated hypotheses. The order is determined by the nature of the project. When the project is concerned with a problem, the problem might be stated followed by the specific aims and hypotheses related to it. When the project is to make a point, it might be stated and followed by statements of the activities associated with its proof. The order used must be one that reveals the importance and scientific potential of your project.

The Background and Significance section contains groundwork for the proposed specific aims and should be easily related to them. Do not write the literature review as a catalog. Help the reviewer understand the order you perceive by using both transitional and topic sentences. It is critical that this section be a well-ordered and integrated presentation of prior research. This section cannot just be a collection of facts or words: The facts and words must be presented so that they engender and communicate thought.

The Research Methods and Design section should also follow the order begun in the Specific Aims section. Place descriptions of procedures that studies have in common before the individual study descriptions. This overview can then be referred to in each study's presentation, followed by the study's unique variations.

Statistical tests of the hypotheses should be presented in the same order as the hypotheses were presented in the Specific Aims section. A statement linking statistical tests to hypotheses should be included whenever possible. Sometimes this is cumbersome to do because one analysis tests several hypotheses. It is more difficult to elucidate how you expect to arrive at your conclusions when this is the case, but it is nevertheless important to present unambiguous statements for the reviewer, even at the expense of repetition.

Finally, headings can serve as a map of the document for reviewers. Because of this, it is not a good plan to use identical headings in different sections of the project plan. If a reviewer puts your application aside and returns to a page with headings that are duplicated in different sections, there will be confusion about the section being read. Deflect any confusion on the part of the reviewer by using unambiguous headings throughout the proposal.

FOCUS

A competitive proposal is written so that the reviewer remains focused on content and thought. A focused proposal establishes expectations for the reviewer and meets those expectations from the wording of the title to the final conclusion about expected statistical results. Focus is achieved through scrutiny of sentence structure, content, and wording.

Sentence Structure

Because an application is a long document, it should be as easy to read as possible. One way to make reading the document easier is to make the structure of the sentences promote comprehension, and this can be done by beginning multiclause sentences with the most important clause.

Simple Sentence Structure

Simple sentence structure is highly valued by many readers. We are all familiar with the person who begins talking and lets no one else speak. The speaker elaborates elaborations and, without a signal, launches into a new topic. We think of this as talking in semicolons. We have encountered this when we read an application with long, complex sentences, showered with semicolons and allusions to other topics. Sometimes, long sentences cannot be avoided, such as one that includes a list of variables. Keep in mind that simple sentences are not necessarily short, but they should have only one independent clause (Watkins & Dillingham, 1992). However, do not complicate the sentence by describing the variables within the sentence. Use additional sentences for elaboration. Some repetition will occur, but it is better to repeat than to entangle the reader in multiple clauses. Another reason for avoiding long sentences, other than the difficulty of sorting out such a sentence, is that it can easily give the impression that the investigator has not yet reached the nugget of his or her thought. Crisp and direct statements are easily understood, give an application an orderly and structured appearance, and permit the thoughts to dominate rather than the words.

Active Voice

Active voice sentences are more interesting and simpler, and they are recommended whenever possible. Active verbs aid understanding because they communicate who is acting. We do not suggest that only active voice sentences be used, but that you consider using them whenever possible.

COMPLETENESS AND CONTENT

Each primary section (e.g., Specific Aims, Introduction, Background and Significance, or Research Methods and Design) should include enough information to permit the reviewer to make inferences about the project. Although each section presents one aspect of the project, each section should contain enough information from the other sections to enable the reviewer to piece together the application's logic and argument. When this is done, each section can be read alone with a high level of understanding. Each section of the research plan has its own purpose, but all sections are a part of the same application. The Specific Aims or Introduction sections provide limited information about the theoretical underpinning of the project but clearly state the hypotheses. The Literature Review section expands the underlying arguments for the hypotheses and contributes further information about the scientific content of the project. However, to be persuasive, this section must also mention the hypotheses or questions posed. The Research Methods and Design section outlines how the data will be collected and analyzed to test the hypotheses that were presented in the first section.

Each paragraph should contain sufficient information for the reviewer to correctly interpret sentences within the context of the application. Because some reviewers are not experts in your topic area, it is important to provide more information than might be required in a journal article. You might keep in mind that communication can be fragile because each reader draws conclusions based on his or her experiences. A project application is not the place to use slang, culturally-driven expressions, or unnecessary jargon.

Another area in which content and completeness are important is comparisons. Be sure that whenever comparison words are used, the sentence is completed. Although it seems that no one would write a sentence such as, "There are a greater number of x cells," understood comparisons are commonly used. In a project plan it is important to complete sentences so that there is no question about the comparison. Comparison sentences should clarify what is being compared with what: "There are a greater number of x cells than y cells." Implied comparisons might be acceptable when all reviewers have equal knowledge, but they still can cause confusion.

Words That Influence Content Perception

Some words assist in directing a reader's attention and conclusions and others distract. The following are some examples of word usage that influence how a reader views a document.

The Words "Former" and "Latter"

The content of each sentence, paragraph, or section should be as complete as possible. The words "former" and "latter" should be avoided. Using these words requires a reviewer to search for the former or latter. In the same vein is the custom of referring readers to "Chapter 1, Figure 1." If it is important that the reviewer see the figure again, repeat it! If it is not valuable enough to be repeated, then choose the place where it needs to be included and handle future situations differently. Reviewers are not interested in "ten-finger documents"—documents in which it takes all ten fingers and perhaps more to keep track of all the places the writer sends the reader. Keep information together. If, however, it is not possible to eliminate references to other parts of the document, it is preferred that they be descriptive, such as "Chapter 1, Figure 1." The need for descriptive references places a premium on using meaningful paragraph headings because they act as guideposts for a reader.

Words Such as "Strength" and "Shortcoming"

Use the words "strength" or "advantage" and "weakness" or "shortcoming" when these words characterize the topic of your discussion. Do not assume the reviewer will correctly label procedures, studies, or analyses as a strength, weakness, or shortcoming. The inclusion of these words elaborates the information provided and provides a check for the reviewer of his or her own conclusions. These kinds of words, which direct the reviewer's view toward your own, are important to accurately judge the scientific contribution of your project.

WORD USAGE

Jargon

One of the meanings assigned to jargon by Webster is the technical terminology of a special activity or group. Technical terminology is used to communicate precisely and efficiently within a scientific or other specialty area. In our opinion, it is best to avoid jargon in a project proposal.

Whether or not jargon is inappropriate depends upon the application's audience. For example, if a proposal is written in response to a Request for Application (RFA) or a Request for Proposal (RFP), both situations in which the reviewers will be very knowledgeable in the area of research targeted, jargon is acceptable. In fact, the use of jargon in communication with individuals within a scientific area is appropriate because of the fine distinctions it makes possible. However, with the current climate of multidisciplinary research, jargon should be used only when there is no other choice.

Synonyms

Using synonyms usually produces a more interesting document than one in which there is much word repetition. However, the use of synonyms in a project plan can result in ambiguity. Individuals outside a particular area of investigation might not know when differences are not important or when a new variable or concept is being introduced. For example, the words "rural," "nonurban," and "Appalachian" might refer to the same group of people, or they might not. In this instance, good communication is achieved by the use of only one of the terms throughout the application. A reviewer might wonder when one of the other terms appears: "Is this another group? I don't remember seeing it mentioned before. Did I miss it? Guess I'd better go back and hunt for it." This is not the way to create a positive frame of mind in the reviewer.

In summary, because of the confusion that can arise from use of synonyms for words that are integral to the science of a proposal, we recommend that they not be used. In this case variety is not welcome. Using the same word again and again and again makes it clear what is being studied, the methods used, or the analysis proposed. The science presented will be clearly visible and more likely to excite the reviewer's intellect than if obscured by attempts at verbal variety.

Simple Words

We recommend simple words. Long, complex sentences filled with multisyllabic words are usually tiring. The purpose of the words in an application is to *communicate good science*. Reviewers want to learn about the project, not about the breadth and depth of your vocabulary. Each sentence should be crafted to express ideas and precipitate thought. The easier an application is to read, the more possible it is for the reviewer to maintain a positive state of mind, especially those for whom English is a second language and those in other scientific areas.

Unnecessary Words

Whenever possible eliminate the use of unnecessary words. The following are some examples from Strunk and White (1979):

the question as to whether	whether (the question whether)
there is no doubt but that	no doubt (doubtless)
used for fuel purposes	used for fuel
he is a man who	he
in a hasty manner	hastily
this is a subject that	this subject
His story is a strange one.	His story is strange.
the reason why is that	because
owing to the fact that	since (because)
in spite of the fact that	though (although)
the fact that he had not succeeded	his failure
the fact that I had arrived	my arrival

Because the writing in a project plan carries a heavy communication burden, use your judgment about what constitutes wordiness or use of unnecessary words. It is unwise to "sacrifice concreteness and vividness for conciseness and brevity" (Watkins & Dillingham, 1992, p. 38).

Avoid Padding

Padding may be the function of a writing style that uses unnecessary words, such as those discussed in the previous section, redundancy, or both unnecessary words and redundancy. Redundancy is repetition of the same thought, not the use of synonyms for concepts integral to the project. We recommend that you say it once and say it right. If you find it necessary to write a sentence that starts with, "In other words. . . . " suspect that your writing may be redundant. However, if you cannot communicate your thought any other way, be redundant. When redundancy arises from an attempt to communicate a thought before it is completely formed, it can be removed during editing. However, be wary about editing apparently redundant statements without thinking about them and their context. Perhaps the statement needs to be elaborated, not repeated, for the reviewer to grasp its meaning and significance.

Do not include extra material in your plan because you think it is too short. If it is short, and if you have included all pertinent information, leave it that way. Reviewers usually do not complain about a short well-written project plan that communicates the science adequately—in short, meets Reif-Lehrer's (1989, p. 87) suggestion that "the reader wants the *maximum* information in the *minimum* number of words." Review your plan and assure yourself that you have included everything as completely as required, but do not add material simply to make it longer.

A project plan that exceeds the page limits should be checked for padding. The excess length might be the result of redundancy, use of unnecessary words, or the inclusion of tangential material. After eliminating redundancy and unnecessary word use, check the material carefully for tangential material. The development of a tightly designed project incorporates numerous tangential information threads. These threads deepen the investigator's comprehension of the project, enabling him or her to present it in a clear concise manner, but they are not, of themselves, important to the reviewer. Including them in the document can give an unfocused appearance to the plan and can contribute significantly to the project's page length. Be vigilant and avoid including material of this nature.

ACTION STRATEGIES

Spell Check

Be sure to use the word processing spell check program, but remember that *it only checks spelling.* Sometimes the wrong word is entered but spelled correctly. Proofread the application yourself and have someone else proofread it to be sure that the words are what you intend and that they are spelled correctly.

Grammar Check

The application's grammar need not be perfect, but it should be good. Good grammar helps communicate good science. Poor grammar can be a barrier to understanding and to the reviewer's positive frame of mind. Use one of the word processing grammar packages on your application, or request a grammar consultant to read your application, and follow the suggestions that will improve communication with the reviewer.

Monitor the Application's First Impression

Give yourself a slight edge by making sure that the first impression your application makes is a good one. First impressions can become hard-core reality, whether they be favorable or unfavorable. Follow the funding source rules for structure. Be sure that the application is complete, that the entire application meets high standards of neatness and accuracy, and that a brief perusal reveals that it is well-organized and easy to access.

Write Drafts

Write drafts! Ordinarily it is not possible to write more than a few drafts, sometimes only two, but that does not mean that the first draft must be the first written thoughts. Fortunately most of us do a lot of writing, including memos and summaries for collaborators as the project plan develops. Save these materials and edit them. Your ideas will take shape more quickly if they are subjected to scrutiny in written form. Any project notes should be saved. They might qualify for inclusion in the first draft of the proposal.

Review Books on Writing

Some of the books we have found useful are listed below. If you have a favorite that you have not used in a while, dust it off and review what are believed to be effective writing habits and styles.

Shertzer, M. (1986). *The elements of grammar.* New York: Macmillan.
Strunk, W., Jr., & White, E. B. (1979). *The elements of style* (3rd ed.). New York: Macmillan.
Watkins, F. C., & Dillingham, W. B. (1992). *Practical English handbook* (9th ed.). Dallas: Houghton Mifflin.

REFERENCES

Price, J. (1981). *Thirty days to more powerful writing: A step-by-step method for developing a more dynamic writing style.* New York: Fawcett Columbine.
Strunk, W., Jr., & White, E. B. (1979). *The elements of style* (3rd ed.). New York: Macmillan.
Watkins, F. C., & Dillingham, W. B. (1992). *Practical English handbook* (9th ed.). Dallas: Houghton Mifflin.

PART VI

Checking for Infractions

Preparing for the Audience

14

Seeing It Through the Reviewers' Eyes

Previous chapters have been concerned with specific aspects of an application. This chapter provides an overview of the details of an application and a checklist that can be used to track your progress in completing the application. An unstated theme running throughout the previous chapters is that a competitive application must be pleasing to the eyes and exciting to the reviewers' intellects. These qualities must hold up under the best and worst reviewing circumstances. Reviewers are scientists who have ongoing research projects, classes to teach, service commitments to meet, and administrative duties or community agencies to administer. The fact that they have volunteered to be reviewers attests to their commitment to scientific endeavors, but it does not mean that they have time on their hands. Some will leisurely review applications, and others will review them under time pressure. Your goal is to write your application so that it is appealing and persuasive, thereby ensuring a good review, even if read under the worst conditions.

This chapter can serve as a "proxy reviewer" for an application. The checklist provided can help locate any gaps and shortcomings in selected

areas. This review can of course be done anytime during project development, but definitely should be done several weeks before the submission
because it is often difficult for an investigator to do a comprehensive review
of the application shortly before submission. After working on the application over the last 6 to 9 months, saturation with the material tempts investigators to skip a final check for gaps or shortcomings. Even though it might
be difficult, do not put it off; be as relentless in completing the application
according to high standards as you are relentless in pursuing good science.
Reap motivation from knowing that filling gaps and eliminating shortcomings improve the application's competitive potential.

FUNDING SOURCE MISSION AND REQUIREMENTS

Review the funding source information to affirm that your research meets
its needs. Keep in mind that a funding source chosen early in the development of an application might not be as appropriate after the application is
complete. Examples of influential changes include the subject pool, the
project costs, overhead costs, and the earliest starting date. Sometimes an
investigator begins to develop an application with a small grant or pilot
project in mind, but as the plan is developed, a greater potential becomes
apparent and a full project results. A comparison of the funding source's
instructions with your final product is time well-spent. It can provide an
opportunity for you to correct deviations or assure yourself that the application meets the structural expectations of reviewers.

PLEASING TO THE EYES

Because the first impression on a reviewer is made by an application's
appearance, take a critical look at your application's appearance. How does
it look? Does it have the appearance a reviewer expects? The more detailed
the funding source instructions, the easier it is to produce an application
that is pleasing to the eyes of reviewers. They have expectations about an
application's appearance, and what you need to do is follow the instructions
to produce an application with that appearance. If detailed instructions are
not provided, use the items presented here for guidance to produce an
application that makes a good first impression.

Cover Page

Funding sources usually require a cover page. Your application may include a form with detailed instructions, or it may simply state the requirements for a cover page in general terms. Instructions, when provided, might give directions about appearance and content.

Check your cover page. Does its appearance coincide with the funding source's instructions? Check the recommendations for type size for the cover page items. Notice that the recommended type size might be different in different parts of the application. Margins on the left, right, top, and bottom might be recommended. The left margin is particularly important to notice because the applications might be bound at the funding source. Title length might be restricted to a certain number of words or characters.

The information required on a cover page fills an information need of the funding source. Complete each item accurately and neatly within the space constraints required. The PI's mailing address must be correct and complete. Unbelievable as it may seem, funding sources have trouble corresponding by mail with investigators because inaccurate addresses are provided. If signatures are required, be sure they are provided in the proper space. A mere glance across this page leaves an impression on all who look at it. Incomplete or sloppily presented information does not make a good impression.

Abstract

Be sure that your abstract follows instructions provided, including the number of words and the type size. If there are no instructions, your abstract should be brief and informative using a moderate type size, 10 to 12 points, and 6 lines per vertical inch.

Personnel Information

Provide all of the personnel information requested. It may not seem reasonable to you, but funding sources have their own databases that require information. Provide whatever is requested, even if it is repetitious from one individual to the next.

Table of Contents

The table of contents provides two kinds of information for the reviewers. It lists the application components and it presents the order in which contents appear in the application. Have you ordered your application materials as outlined in the table of contents provided by the funding source? Check the accuracy of the order and the page numbers. Some funding sources do not permit using page numbers such as 3a, 3b. Under these circumstances, if pages have been added after numbering, all pages must be renumbered and the table of contents modified accordingly. If a form is not provided, include a table of contents that lists each application component and its page number. A complete table of contents aids the efficiency of a reviewer and is appreciated. A table of contents for the project plan is an added feature that is helpful to reviewers. However, this might have to be placed within the page limit of the project plan and, therefore, is usually not provided.

Budget

Review the budget information you have provided for adherence to funding source guidelines and preferences. If a budget form is provided, the information should be neatly typed in the spaces provided. If categories are not applicable, or if there are no dollar amounts, use dashes or write "not applicable" so that it is clear that you have considered the item and have not forgotten to fill it in. Do not forget to include all personnel mentioned in the project. If they are donating their time, indicate that, but do not omit them from the budget. Neatly typed, complete budget pages and a budget justification with paragraph headings create a good impression.

Supporting Documents

PI and Investigator Related

Biographical sketches and information about other external support for projects should receive careful attention. A biographical sketch that has obviously been culled from another application, is barely legible, and has been hurriedly modified to fit the current application will not make a good impression. Check these supporting documents to be certain that they have been prepared as carefully as the project plan, following the guidelines for type size and page limitations. Present the information about other external project funds in a consistent manner. A consistent presentation not only gives the appearance of being easier to use, but is, in fact, easier for the reviewer to use.

Applicant Organization Related

Another set of supporting documents is that related to the PI's organization and the environment in which the project will be conducted. Complete this information as neatly and carefully as the rest of the application. There is no way to tell when a reviewer will look at any one of these pages, and sloppy work on them can form a disastrous impression as easily as will sloppy work on other parts of the application. Neatness and completeness count, and reviewers assume the PI will take responsibility for these matters.

The Project Plan

Have you presented the project plan in the number of pages allowed by the funding source? If there is no recommended page limit, keep in mind that a project plan of 20 to 25 single-spaced pages is usually more welcome than one that is 50 to 100 pages. Most often, if excessive page length results in the return of an application, reviewers do not see it. However, when reviewers do see these applications they might believe that unfair advantage results from accepting the extra pages. In this case a reviewer might return the application, be influenced negatively by the investigator taking license to include more material, or review the document as if it were the appropriate length. The risk of a negative consequence of breaking the page-length rules should not be taken.

Primary headings should coincide with those presented in the instructions. Other headings should be included only to enhance reviewer comprehension. An excessive use of headings is not helpful. Keep in mind that headings are used as markers or guideposts throughout the document, and use them accordingly.

Double spacing between paragraphs and paragraph indentation increase the desirable white space on each page. This makes reading less tiresome, and permits the reviewer's attention to focus on the science. Sometimes investigators just cannot seem to fit their material into the required number of pages without using every bit of space on the page. If you have this problem, try lengthening the lines of type while retaining paragraph indentation and double spacing between paragraphs. Next, if you are still short of space, try using a space and a half between paragraphs. The balance is between including the information and getting the reviewer to be able to comprehend it. With no white space, the investigator may have included the information but has sacrificed the reviewer's attention and positive mood. In general, readers find their attention wandering when confronted with page after page of solid type.

Present legible and well-designed graphs and tables. Captions with type size so small that the letters become dots when reproduced can be a source of frustration for the reviewer.

Produce your final application with technology that is generally available. Although some parts of an application require typewriters, most parts of applications are produced with word processing software and laser printers. However, using a typewriter for the entire document is preferred if a letter quality printer is not available. Do not include low-clarity photographs.

Bind the application as instructed. A common instruction is to submit each copy held together with a rubber band. Bind the application according to instructions, or secure it using a simple method if instructions are not provided. Excessive binding and printing efforts are not necessary and may detract from a favorable impression.

Summary

In summary, the entire research application must be neat. It must conform to type size and spacing instructions, or it must have type size and spacing that make it easy to read. It should be the length expected by the reviewer, and, if there are no instructions, it should be a reasonable length. Keep in mind that you are trying to create a positive mood in the reviewer and hold his or her attention so that a good evaluation of your science is possible.

EXCITING TO THE INTELLECT

Organization

A project plan cannot be intellectually exciting if its organization does not emphasize the arguments leading to your conclusions and the beauty of the methodology and analysis that implement your plan. Unfortunately, there is no template that can be used in organizing a project proposal, outside of that requested by the funding source.

The Specific Aims (Introduction)

Educate the reviewers about your particular topic. State the broad long-term goals of projects in your area. Along with this statement, include a sentence or two about the benefit of your findings, including cost savings or diminution in some misfortune. These two kinds of information presented early in the application allow the reviewer to quickly place your project in context.

The next statement describes what your project will lead to or accomplish. This is an important statement because reviewers may not draw the same conclusions that you draw. It is possible that the specific aims could have several lines of development.

The specific aims, together with the hypotheses or questions generated, are stated next. It is here that the organization can vary. Sometimes it is difficult to decide which aims should be stated first. Sometimes there is no logical connection between aims. What is not questioned is that the hypotheses and questions should be presented either with each specific aim, or following all specific aims in the same order so there is no confusion about which hypotheses or questions are associated with which specific aim. Use your knowledge of the topic area and your project to decide on this organization. Think about the order you select. Consider the pros and cons of alternate arrangements. The organization of this first section is important because it is the model for each succeeding section's organization.

Literature Review

The organization of this section should follow that of the Specific Aims section and the logic of your project. Be sure that your early discussion of the rationale for the proposed project deflects confusion.

The literature for each specific aim should be discussed as a unit if that is possible. If the specific aims stem from a common body of literature, then the relationship between the literature and the specific aims must be clearly presented. Assess whether your discussion of previous research is integrated and fosters comprehension rather than confusion. Be sure that the conclusions you state can be arrived at through following the line of thought presented. Remember, you are the reviewer's guide through the literature as it pertains to your project.

Research Methods and Design

The order of this section is determined by discipline convention, investigator's preference, and the project. Be sure that you do not frustrate a reviewer's expectations by using unconventional arrangements of material. If there are no conventions, review the order you have chosen in light of persuasiveness and interest. The dilemma here is that different scientists have different preferences, but by this stage of application development you are probably fairly familiar with the preferences of those working in the topic area. The minimum to be achieved in this section is an orderly and consistent presentation.

Content

In respect to content, do not make assumptions about what reviewers know. Search your project plan for statements that include jargon or are presented with insufficient groundwork. Assuming it is a well-organized application, the content or lack of content is visible. Have you taken advantage of opportunities to communicate the excitement of your project? Your scientific ability should be demonstrated by your ability to succinctly describe your project, by your past activities, and by the care you give to the application details. Do not give reviewers the impression that you are saying, "Trust me, I am an expert."

Specific Aims (Introduction)

Your project context should be described in a compelling manner. However, exaggerating or overemphasizing the need for your project will jeopardize your credibility. Your statements should be objective and trained on your specific aims because you have chosen a funding source that is already interested in the general area of your project. Review your statement of the influence of your findings on the current state of affairs, and adjust it as required either for over- or understatement.

Check that you have stated the hypotheses or the questions to be answered by your project. In our experience, stating specific aims is not sufficient because specific aims are not tested.

Literature Review

The review must include relevant literature, recent work, and relevant review group member findings. If your topic is one with alternative investigative directions, do not neglect to summarize alternative directions that might be chosen by other investigators and state your arguments for continuing pursuit along your chosen lines. Be sure that you have not included tangential material or asides. Remember, the reviewers are not interested in everything you know: They are interested in how you integrate current and past findings to arrive at your project. Check your presentation to determine if you have included enough of your thinking to reveal your integration method and how it leads to your conclusions. Be sure you have not unwittingly made an unimportant point appear important through the use of multiple examples.

Research Methods and Design

This is the most important section of an application because it describes the way data will be collected. Research conclusions are only as good as the data on which they are based.

Be sure the design is described, not just named. Remember, across disciplines designs might be the same but names might be different, so don't rely on a shorthand of design names. Review, for clarity, your statements about the ability to assess the combined effect of several variables if this is an important feature of a design. The use of variable names to describe the effects is preferable to briefly stating that "the significance of interactions or cross-products will be tested."

Review your presentation of the groups you are proposing to study and their characteristics. Assumptions must not be made about what reviewers know about the characteristics of the chosen group, whether the group is composed of humans, animals, or cultures. Have you included information about recruitment and attrition as appropriate?

Instrumentation can be complex and cumbersome to describe. Review your description to determine if you have provided a sufficient amount of information to enable a reviewer to make judgments about the appropriateness, reliability, and validity of the proposed instruments. If they are the "standard" used by investigators in the area of research, less description is required than if they are not commonly used or cutting edge instruments. Keep in mind that these descriptions need to be presented in ordinary language whenever possible. A full description and complete technical material can be included as an appendix, but the appendix material should be viewed as ancillary information.

Procedure sections should include enough information about procedures so a reviewer could replicate them. Search out summary terms such as standard analysis, participant observation, usual arrangement, computer-entered responses, or usual computer set-up. Provide the series of statements these shorthand descriptions require for replication to be possible. Careful presentation of the details of procedures and their order enables the reviewer to more vividly imagine your project.

Data Management and Analysis

Check all the details of data collection, storage, protection, and management you have presented. Statements like "data were collected" are not sufficient. Detailed information about data collection and its care assures reviewers that data loss is unlikely. Have you assured reviewers that you are aware of the importance of considering threats to data during all project phases?

Succinctly describe all data analyses. Frequently the data collected are not the data that are analyzed. Spell out how you expect to modify data before they are analyzed, and the reasons for those expected modifications. In some areas, data transformations are uncommon; in other areas, specific variables are commonly transformed before analysis. Have you presented sufficient information to assure reviewers that you are aware of conventions and requirements and are competent at data analysis?

To communicate how you intend to test your hypotheses, describe the statistical tests and their power. A brief discussion of the chosen level of power and the calculations are helpful to reviewers.

Now that you have reviewed your entire project plan and the mission of the funding source, review the personnel to be used, the budget required, and the supporting materials.

Personnel, Budget, and Budget Justification

During the application's development, collaborative needs might change from those originally envisioned and discussed. The most dramatic change occurs when an entire section of a project is changed. If you have had regular contact with your collaborators during proposal development, this will be reflected in your final list of key personnel and your budget. Minor modifications in methods and design might also need to be reflected in the budget and budget justification. For example, the percent effort required for investigators might be increased or decreased, or project staff might need to be added. Review the lab work needs, data entry or data collection, and subcontracts such as computer programming or statistical analysis required by the final proposal. It is critical that personnel, budget, and budget justification match the proposed project needs.

Supporting Materials

Your biographical sketch and those of your co-investigators are presented as evidence of your ability to conduct the proposed project. Review these to be certain that the material is relevant to the final research proposal.

The available resources and the environment should also be adequate to complete the project. Do not forget minor project changes that might represent a major change in required resources. An example might be the addition of a lab test that needs to be done through a subcontract arrangement rather than internally.

ADMINISTRATIVE APPROVALS

Early in the project development, you need to determine your organization's procedure for submitting an application for external funding. Check the forms you have completed, and the list of steps and signatures required before the application can be mailed to the funding source. Be sure that the materials you have prepared are correct so they will move through the system smoothly without time-consuming questions and corrections, and that there is sufficient time for approval signatures. If there is no time for all approval signatures, determine the procedure used to facilitate the application submission on time.

ACTION STRATEGIES

Request Notification of Receipt

Include a self-addressed stamped postcard with the application, requesting that it be dated and returned to you when the funding source receives the application. Often the funding source will include the number it assigns the application. This can be useful information should the need arise for communicating about it with the funding source.

Do a Final Check of the Application

Use the checklist shown in Table 14.1 to assure yourself that you have written as competitive an application as possible. Each item on the checklist is accompanied by two blank lines. One set of lines should be used to enter the page number of the application on which you find the item or NA if not applicable to this application. On the second line, check those items that have been forgotten or need additional writing. The checklist is not an exhaustive list. However, it will serve to remind you of the items that your application must include to be competitive. As you think of additional items, add them at the end of the list.

Table 14.1   General Checklist

Item	Application Page	Yes-No
I. Funding Source Mission		
A. Is the research topic or purpose(s) within the mission of the chosen funding source?	_____	_____
1. Do you need to call the funding source to verify?	_____	_____
B. Is the breadth of the project in line with that expected by the funding source?	_____	_____
C. Is there confidence that the research goals are worth financial support?	_____	_____
II. Pleasing to the Eye		
A. Cover Page		
1. Is the correct type size used on all pages?	_____	_____
2. Is the title the right length?	_____	_____
3. Has your full and correct address been entered?	_____	_____
4. Have all forms been signed in all required places?	_____	_____
B. Have abstract instructions been followed?	_____	_____
C. Has all requested personal information been provided?	_____	_____
D. Are the items in the table of contents and the page numbers correct?	_____	_____
E. Budget and Budget Justification		
1. Has the requested budget detail been provided?	_____	_____
2. Have all project expenses been shown?	_____	_____
3. Have the allowable cost-of-living or merit increases been factored in?	_____	_____
4. Is the budget realistic for the project proposed?	_____	_____
5. Can reviewers link expenses to project procedures?	_____	_____
6. Are the calculations correct?	_____	_____
F. Supporting Documents		
1. PI and Investigator Information		
a. Are biographical sketches for all key personnel included?	_____	_____
b. Is other project funding for all investigators reported?	_____	_____
2. Applicant Organization Information		
a. Has all requested information on the ability and willingness of your organization to support your project been included?	_____	_____

continued

Table 14.1   Continued

Item	Application Page	Yes-No
b. Are all required assurance numbers included and correct?	_____	_____
G. The Project Plan		
1. Have the required page limitations been observed?	_____	_____
2. Do the paragraph and section headings help direct the reader?	_____	_____
3. Is there white space on the pages?	_____	_____
4. Are the graphs and tables legible?	_____	_____
5. Do graphs and tables conform to funding source restrictions?	_____	_____
III. *Exciting to the Intellect*		
A. Organization		
1. Specific Aims or Introduction		
a. Has a rationale been presented?	_____	_____
b. Has a broad long-term goal been presented?	_____	_____
c. Have clear specific aims been presented?	_____	_____
d. Have hypotheses or questions been included?	_____	_____
2. Literature Review		
a. Does the literature review follow the same information pattern as the specific aims or introduction?	_____	_____
b. Is the material presented in an orderly way leading the reviewer to draw your conclusions?	_____	_____
c. Have you avoided a catalog-like presentation of facts?	_____	_____
3. Project Methods and Design		
a. Is this section ordered in the way customary for your discipline or as requested by the funding source?	_____	_____
b. Can the reviewer link components of this section to the literature review?	_____	_____
c. Is the focus and direction of the project evident?	_____	_____
d. Is the relationship between this section and the hypotheses or questions evident?	_____	_____
B. Content		
1. Does each of the following sections present the material in a persuasive and easy to read fashion with jargon used only when required for clarity?		
a. Specific Aims or Introduction	_____	_____
b. Literature Review	_____	_____
c. Research Design and Methods	_____	_____

continued

Table 14.1   Continued

Item	Application Page	Yes-No
2. Does each of the following sections provide sufficient information?		
a. Specific Aims or Introduction	_____	_____
(1) Statement of how the research fits into the scientific knowledge base	_____	_____
(2) Clearly stated hypotheses or questions	_____	_____
b. Literature Review		
(1) Has the review been complete enough to conclude that the proposed project has not already been done?	_____	_____
(2) Does the review have the proper emphasis for the proposed project?	_____	_____
(3) Have you cited your own work and placed it in its proper place?	_____	_____
(4) Have you avoided fanning the flames of controversy?	_____	_____
c. Project Design and Analysis		
(1) Do the project design and purpose match?	_____	_____
(2) Are enough observations included to support the planned analysis?	_____	_____
(3) Has a statement about the power of your statistical tests been included?	_____	_____
(4) Have the subjects been described in sufficient detail?	_____	_____
(5) Have requirements for inclusion of minority and women subjects been addressed?	_____	_____
(6) Have the procedures been described in sufficient detail and without recourse to jargon?	_____	_____
(7) Have data management procedures been included?	_____	_____
d. Has the preliminary or pilot study section been completed?	_____	_____
(1) Has the preliminary or pilot work been related to the proposed project?	_____	_____
e. Personnel, Budget, and Budget Justification and Supporting Materials. Are these documents accurate and comprehensive?		
(1) Personnel Section	_____	_____
(2) Budget, First Year Detailed	_____	_____
(3) Budget, Additional Years	_____	_____
(4) Budget Justification	_____	_____
(5) Biographical Sketches	_____	_____
(6) Resources and Environment	_____	_____

continued

Table 14.1   Continued

Item	Application Page	Yes-No
f. Personnel, Budget, and Budget Justification and Supporting Materials. Do the contents of these documents reflect all changes that have occurred since project development began?		
(1) Personnel Section	_____	_____
(2) Budget, First Year Detailed	_____	_____
(3) Budget, Additional Years	_____	_____
(4) Budget Justification	_____	_____
(5) Biographical Sketches	_____	_____
(6) Resources and Environment	_____	_____
g. Has sufficient information about administrative support been provided to persuade reviewers that administrative matters will not be a barrier to the project's completion?	_____	_____

PART VII

The Reviewers' Decision

Endgame

15

Funded

Life after funding is often not as expected by new principal investigators. This chapter discusses some of the new responsibilities of a funded investigator and some of the administrative duties associated with receiving an award. Several principles are also presented that we believe can be most useful in helping to achieve the objective of a successful project and grant. The chapter begins with an overview of the importance of the grant award statement and reviews the limitations associated with receiving a grant. Possible budget arrangements are presented in which new investigators will most probably find themselves. Rules and regulations about personnel and equipment that seem to be a straitjacket for some investigators are also highlighted. Finally, action strategies are presented that emphasize a role that we describe as the "small business manager," which we believe will be most useful for the new investigator to assume.

After waiting from 9 to 12 months since submitting your project application, you receive notification of your award from the funding source. This is usually the culmination of a series of communications with them. The first communication was probably a notice from the funding source that your application was received and assigned to a review group. If you thought the review group assignment appropriate, your next communication with the funding source was probably after the application was reviewed. Most funding sources inform PIs of the status of their application after the final review and when the application's disposition has been decided. Others provide information about the scientific review before the funding decision has been made. Many investigators initiate communication with the funding source personnel to keep abreast of the status of their application so that they are a step ahead should a resubmission be necessary. In the federal government's peer review system, the application is next reviewed by the Institutes' National Advisory Council. For those grants that are approved, it then becomes the responsibility of the Institutes' program staff to fund grant applications on the basis of the percentile scores received. The strongest application, the application with the lowest percentile score, receives first funding within the funding area; funding then moves down the list of approved applications as far as available funds will allow.

Awards are made in amounts deemed appropriate by the funding source. The amount of the award might be for the amount requested in the application, for the amount requested less some percent, or for the amount requested, less some amount that has been negotiated with the principal investigator. Budget reductions, whether they are done unilaterally by the funding source or negotiated with the PI, pose a dilemma for many investigators because most often proposed budgets do not have enough elasticity to absorb these reductions. After having discussions and agonizing before the award is made, you make budget cuts to accommodate the budget reductions and in the process realize that you could modify your project. So with this reality, you recognize that next time you'll make sure to include all inflation factors to assure that cuts will not place your proposed project or research "in harm's way." You had not expected to do business in this strange way—that is, proposing an adequate budget that is subsequently cut thereby placing your project in completion jeopardy. When submitting applications in the future, the strategy adopted to handle this situation depends on the project, the PI, and applicant organizational setting.

The notice of grant award is the official announcement to the principal investigator from the funding source that a grant application has been funded. This notification is delivered by telephone, mail, or both, although we have heard of instances in which there was only a telephone call, followed by a check. These instances, by and large, involved funding from foundations. However the award notice is made, to paraphrase of one our colleagues, "Now the fun begins."

NOTICE OF GRANT AWARD

Because the information in the grant award directly influences project expenditures, we will closely examine the actual written grant award statement. We will use the Public Health Service Notice of Grant Award as the example that is used for NIH grants. The first thing to keep in mind is that the *grant award is not made to the principal investigator*. The award is made to the principal investigator's institution—the university or the community agency. The money is not the principal investigator's and is subject to rules and regulations, both federal and institutional. Both issues are important. Because "your" grant is awarded to the institution, you need to be aware of the limitations that this places on you as the principal investigator, most of which relate to fiscal matters. For example, if you decide to move to another institution, you will need to negotiate moving "your" funded research. Both you and the institution that received the award could be losers if an agreement about moving the study is not reached. In fact, in the worst-case scenario, the award would terminate.

The award statement contains the following kinds of information that are most important. The grant number is the identifier that will be used to refer to your grant throughout the funding period. It is our recommendation that you use this number on all correspondence by clearly putting it near the top of all written materials. The first letters of the grant number indicate the type of award (for example, RO means research), followed by a unique identifier for your grant and a number for the first year (-01 means first year, -02 means second year, etc.) and for subsequent grant years until the grant terminates. The date of the project period for the total grant period, which is usually 3 to 5 years, and the dates for the current budget period (first year) are also included on the award statement. The approved budget gives the line-item budget for important items, including salaries and wages, fringe benefits, consultant costs, equipment, supplies, travel, patient care, alterations and renovations, consortium/contractual costs, and, if appropriate, costs related to training for training grants.

The funding level for each grant year is specified on the award statement. This is the total direct cost amount; the indirect costs are added to the direct

costs. Indirect costs are computed on the base amount of the grant award for the grant period and are paid to the university for each yearly period. Any restrictions on how funds can be spent, or options for carrying them over to future years, are indicated.

Both the grants management specialist at the funding institute and the NIH Institute's Program Official are listed on the award. These people are the primary contacts for the principal investigator. The grants management specialist is responsible for all fiscal and budget matters related to the grant. If there are questions or issues related to budget changes, purchasing, or changing line items, they should be addressed to the grants management specialist. These changes should be discussed initially with both the program project officer and the grants management specialist, and a copy of the request for change should be sent to the program official. The program official, who is responsible for working with the principal investigator, can act as an advocate for the project, and can be used as a sounding board to discuss issues and possible changes that need to be made to the study or the protocol.

The Notice of Grant Award is signed by the chief of the grants management branch, who is the fiscal officer of the awarding NIH Institute. The chief of the grants management branch also has responsibility for fiscal matters and supervises the Institutes' grants management specialists. Special terms and conditions may also be attached to the grant award; these statements pinpoint additional issues related to receipt of funding and should receive attention.

In summary, the Notice of Grant Award presents the dates for the grant period, gives the approved budget, and can include specific terms and conditions related to the grant, in addition to specifying the amount of the indirect costs included in the grant award. This is the official notice sent by the funding source that the award has been made, and includes both the program and the fiscal contacts for the funded grant. Remember, a PI is not a free agent in using the approved funding identified in the Notice of Grant Award.

PRIOR APPROVAL

Limitations are placed on grantees by the Public Health Service for NIH grants, and this can also be the case for other funding organizations. Some budget categories are restricted to expenditures only within the original application, unless prior approval is received for increasing or decreasing these budget categories. This regulation clearly might influence the kinds of modifications a PI might want to make in a project plan to accommodate a smaller than requested award.

Because failure to obtain prior approval could result in cost disallowances (Public Health Service, 1990), it is important that a new PI learn how to work within these restrictions. These limitations pertain to direct costs but have nothing to do with indirect costs because the indirect cost rate is established for your institution.

On an NIH-funded grant, prior approval by the NIH is necessary for some changes requested by the principal investigator. These regulations also apply to all Department of Health and Human Services grants, but they vary by the type of grant award (i.e., research, construction, training, etc.). Contracts, because they are developed by the government to obtain a specific product or service, are usually more tightly controlled, and billing statements must specify the exact amount of the expenditure for the billing period, usually monthly or quarterly.

The following areas (Public Health Service, 1990) that need prior approval before budget changes can be made are presented here to give specific examples of areas where the principal investigator will need to receive prior approval if changes are made. A key to keep in mind here is that, if there are doubts about the need for approval of changes, we recommend that the assigned grants management officer identified on the NIH award statement be contacted. The following areas are presented for research grants and serve as examples.

- *Change in Scope of the Project or Research Objectives.* This includes major changes in the aims, objectives, or goals. For research grants this includes changing the scope of the research objectives, modifying the research objectives, changing the approved use of animals or humans, shifting emphasis from one disease to another, applying a new technology, transferring the performance of substantive performance to a third party, changing key personnel whose expertise is critical, significant rebudgeting, or incurring new patient care costs.

- *Change in Principal Investigator.* A change in the principal investigator must be approved if the principal investigator is absent for a period of 3 months or more. This request for change must be approved in writing.

- *Changes of Grantee Organization.* A change must receive prior approval.

- *Award Terms and Conditions.* Deviations from the special award conditions stated in the Notice of Grant Award need prior approval.

- *Closely Related Work.* If this work is also funded by the Public Health Service, certain expenditures must receive prior approval.

- *Audiovisuals and Publications.* Approval is needed if costs exceed $25,000 for a single audiovisual or for a single printed publication.

- *Preaward Costs Incurred 90 Days Prior to Award.* There are no federal obligations to pay these costs.

- *Drawings, Specifications for Alterations, and Renovations Over $50,000.* Alterations and renovations may not exceed the lesser of $150,000 or 25% of the total direct costs for the award for 3 years.

- *Indemnification Against Third Parties.* Prior approval must be obtained for any indemnification not covered by insurance.

- *Capital Expenditures for Land and Buildings.* Prior approval must be obtained for these expenditures.

- *Retroactive Approval May Be Requested.* Approval may be requested retroactively only if several conditions are met, including the following: The transaction would have been approved if requested in advance, the transaction is approved by an official who has such responsibility, and the organization agrees to institute controls to insure that prior approval requirements are met in the future.

- *Extensions of the Budget Period.* Approval is needed other than the extension of the final budget period for up to one year beyond the original termination date on the Notice of Grant Award.

In summary, we want to stress the fact that the above areas needing prior approval for changes are presented for NIH research grants as examples. It is important to note that prior approval is needed for any major modifications related to changing the principal investigator, shifting major budget categories, renovating, exceeding $25,000 in printing and publication expenses, or extending the length of time of the award.

INDIRECT COSTS

Indirect costs are of interest to the principal investigator because oftentimes a portion of these indirect costs can be returned to the principal investigator for support of further research. Such policies are dependent upon the applicant organization and are frequently unwritten. Indirect costs have also been used as incentives in certain organizations.

TIMING

Getting started in a timely fashion once a grant has been awarded is critical. Activities related to beginning a project can seem overwhelming. The project timeline you presented in the application can be a very useful tool at this time. It is important to develop project timelines, especially with 12-month or longer grants, so that activities are perceived as an orderly progression rather than as an overwhelming, unrelated mass. Some examples of the categories in which start-up work must be done are personnel, internal budget arrangements, space, and equipment.

Personnel

We believe that the most appropriate advice we can give in the area of hiring staff is to start as quickly as possible after the award is received. If the number of staff requested in the application includes existing staff or a limited number of new staff, timing could be less of a problem than might be anticipated if all project staff need to be hired. A new PI must learn the procedures for acquiring the personnel required for the project. For example, even though new staff positions are written into the application, hiring might be carried out within the rules and personnel policies of the organization receiving the grant. A PI, therefore, must develop position descriptions acceptable to the personnel department, get the position classified at salary levels commensurate with the tasks, write advertisements to attract the appropriate types of skilled people to meet the project's aims, and, finally, interview those who apply. Part of the interview process involves understanding and explaining employee benefits and working hours as well as interpreting job expectations and duties. Establishing expectations to get work completed goes hand-in-hand with being a supervisor. It may be easier to establish expectations than to have those expectations be met. Perhaps supervisory training could be useful. This phase of the project can be difficult if there are delays, which more frequently than not seem to occur.

Universities and other organizations may also add an additional wrinkle during times of flat or constricting budgets. This wrinkle is the need to hire internal candidates for positions before going outside the institution. This is compounded with broad personnel department classifications schemes that make job titles like "research assistant" so broad that research assistants are assumed to be able to work in most, if not all, settings that involve any kind of research. Thus applications from a gaggle of internal candidates may need to be reviewed and interviews may have to be held. These internal candidates may or may not have the expertise or experience appropriate for the funded project. However, to meet the organization's personnel rules, these personnel procedures must be followed if a principal investigator wants to fill the positions funded by the grant.

Be forewarned that personnel department policies may prohibit employing the best person for the job. Sometimes after interviews are completed and the candidate most qualified to carry out the position duties is selected, the organization is unable to authorize the salary level needed for the person on the basis of education, experience, and qualifications. Thus, even though the notice of grant award includes a salary level that is adequate, personnel policies do not allow for the needed level of payment. This dilemma has been resolved creatively in some instances by granting exceptions, but in other cases the selected, qualified individuals are not hired. This usually leaves a bitter taste for the new investigator. Thus, even though money is available from the funding organization, this does not guarantee that staff can be hired at that level of pay.

Internal Budget Arrangements

For clarity of presentation, internal budget arrangements have been separated from external budget arrangements. For this purpose, internal arrangements are those activities within the investigator's own organization. Internal arrangements may be complicated. For example, we have learned through our own experiences that establishing an account number in many organizations can be difficult. The account number in universities is the fiscal accounting point or cost center that is used to charge all project-related expenditures. If an account number has not been established, then there is no mechanism for encumbering costs, and a project is "dead in the water" until an account number is established.

The critical internal issue here is: Who keeps track of the project's funds? One of the best ways to research this issue is to find out who sets up the account numbers and then ask who is responsible for the expenditures related to the account. You may discover that your signature has authority for expenditures. However, more than likely a business manager has final budget authority. What you need to remember is that you are not a free agent—you will have responsibilities within definite fiscal rules and limitations. In other words, we recommend that you not go out and charge something without knowing what you could be getting yourself into.

Space

Space can also be a limiting or enhancing factor. If plentiful space is available for the project, then an important barrier is surmounted. Issues related to space seem to be more complicated for university settings than for community agencies. It has been our experience in working with community agencies that after funding is available, community agencies can enter into leases with limited red tape. Universities, on the other hand, to assure that there are no conflicts of interest, usually have a number of regulations related to renting space if it cannot be obtained within the confines of the university. Required clearances may include signatures from university administrators at various levels such as "property management," with possible approval by the Board of Trustees or another group that advertises the specifications for the space in the approved mechanism, visits sites with property management, and selects the space.

On the other hand, renovations or changes in laboratory set-up may be needed, thereby involving a variety of approvals about which the new investigator may not be knowledgeable. In addition to space, equipment and furniture may need to be bought. This may also mean procurement through specified agents or vendors, depending on the organizational setting.

These chains of events are probably not representative of any one reality, but they could possibly take place and they do take time to resolve. And time is something a new investigator must not feel comfortable about wasting, even though these are the usual events that must take place to get a project established. We again recommend an implementation plan that includes a project timeline. Some of the application timetable development strategies suggested in Chapter 12 can also be used to develop a project timeline.

Equipment

In most formal organizations, there are rules related to procuring equipment. These rules were developed to provide protection for those who might take advantage of the system and provide a framework for the investigator.

It is probably of little surprise to the new investigator that the equipment purchased on the grant is the property of the organization rather than of the investigator(s), and some funding sources retain ownership of equipment purchased with their awards. Many organizations are very efficient at having the new investigator face this reality; others do not do it as well. One of the ways the organization does this is by placing property tags on all equipment. Whichever way this is handled organizationally, the investigator must learn and follow those rules that could have an impact on the project. There might also be equipment needs related to the project that require special purchases or ongoing purchases. These purchases usually need to be made through an established process that can involve writing specifications, receiving bids, and formally reviewing the bids for external purchases. This may also be the case for the rental of space and of other materials that are not purchased.

ACTION STRATEGIES

The following action strategies are presented to provide what we believe are useful approaches to help the new investigator to excel and be successful.

Get Acquainted With What You Promised

After funding is received, "All the chickens come home to roost." After you celebrate, you soon discover that you must now do what you promised in the application. Wow! What did you say you would do? It's probably been a considerable time since you prepared the application, so you reread the procedures section. Often PIs are surprised by what they find. The problem is either that the procedures section is not detailed enough or that it is now outdated given the state of the knowledge and/or newly developed procedures. So, like others faced with the same situation, you think and talk about your dilemma. You take time to prepare changes, further specify procedures, and discuss these changes with your program project officer. This may be a beginning of other modifications you will need to make as the study progresses. The overall strategy must be to get the project going as quickly as possible.

Taking on the Role of a Small Business Manager

Small business manager? What's that got to do with getting a funded project going? We believe it has a great deal to do with it. In fact, the more we've thought about it, the more we are convinced that taking on the attitude and associated behaviors of a small business manager can help both new and established investigators be most successful in achieving their project aims.

We selected the small business analogy because it seems to fit best with the kind of thinking that we believe will make the new investigator most successful. The analogy does not fit perfectly, but it emphasizes the kinds of behaviors that we believe are successful. For example, the small business manager has to operate within the limitations established by U.S. legal code. A principal investigator also has to operate within those limitations, but also with a number of other rules and regulations in either the university or agency setting that are more confining and restricting.

The newly funded investigator must focus on getting the project underway and developed within a reasonable timeframe with the level of resources available. Start-up time must be limited by necessity. Also, the study aims provide the goals and focus for activities. When a new investigator thinks like a small business manager, he or she does not wait for things to happen, but makes them happen. This action-oriented role must not only be used for the project but also must be applied to relationships within the organization to get things accomplished in a timely manner.

A PI of a funded project must, like a small business executive, wear many hats, and wear them effectively. A PI must be a manager, a supervisor, a purchaser, an accountant, and last but not least a scientist.

Develop and Follow an Implementation Timeline

Taking time to develop a timeline for implementing the project activities that are managerial provides a way for you to think through primary issues and potential problems. Because a timeline ties actions and activities with time, it can go a long way toward highlighting how some of the stress and potential strain that accompany the project's beginning and maturity can be eased.

Investigate Your Obligations and Ask About Your Autonomy

Take time to talk with others about the rules of getting funded and how others have coped with this situation. It is our suggestion that you might want to engage in these discussions at your institution with funded project personnel as well as with those you may know in other organizations. These conversations will direct you to the people and positions in the organizational resources described in Chapter 4 that are required for you to successfully conduct your project.

Receiving an award, whether it be a grant or a contract, creates legal relationships. When the award is for a grant, "the institution that employs the principal investigator is the grantee and is legally responsible for the scientific and financial conduct of the grant. The institution, not the principal investigator, 'owns' the grant. The principal investigator is responsible for conducting the science but also may have certain financial responsibilities, such as ensuring that funds from one grant are not used to purchase equipment to be used on another grant. Most cases involving alleged financial improprieties on the part of the principal investigators can be traced to a total lack of understanding of the rules that govern federal grants ... if you are going to earn your living through a specific type of legal relationship, you should understand that relationship" (Charrow, 1993).

REFERENCES

Charrow, R. P. (1993). A primer on research ethics: Learning to cope with federal regulations of research. *Journal of NIH Research, 5,* 76-78.

U.S. Department of Health and Human Services, Public Health Service. (1990, October). *Grants Management Policy* (DHHS Publication No. [OASH] 90-50.000 [Rev.]). Washington, DC: U.S. Government Printing Office.

16

Not Funded

If you don't get funded the first time, try, try, and try again. Three times is probably the most resubmissions anyone should attempt. Revising and resubmitting an application is easier than preparing an original submission in some ways and harder in others. It is easier because the bulk of the project has already been written in the form required by the funding source. But it is harder because the revisions require the PI to think again about the project, and to think in a way that is directed by the reviewers' comments and perceptions. Finally, it is difficult simply because criticism precipitates emotional reactions, no matter how experienced the investigator. This chapter presents some guidance for interpreting the reviewers' comments and for rewriting an application to be resubmitted. Keep in mind that sometimes projects are funded on the first submission, but many of them are funded only after resubmission.

REACTIONS TO REVIEWERS' COMMENTS

Throughout a professional career each of us faces criticism from a variety of sources. The way we respond to criticism depends upon the source of the criticism, the importance to us of what is criticized, and whether the criticism occurs in public or in private. Over time we learn to cope with criticism. If it is unfair or unjustified, it is ignored; if it arises out of ignorance, it is taken lightly; and if it is warranted, we try to learn from it.

The reviewers' comments are from an important source and are of great importance to the principal investigator. Therefore, many investigators are pushed outside their usual coping systems. The reaction to receiving the reviewers' comments has been labeled "the pink sheet syndrome" after the pink paper on which the NIH prints the reviewers' comments (Fuller, 1982). When your application receives a favorable score and is funded, it is difficult to read the reviewers' comments with emotional detachment. However, when the score places the application in the not-funded group, emotional detachment is even more difficult and often impossible. The reactions are understandable when the amount of time, effort, and creativity that goes into an application is considered. PIs are usually intellectually attached to the project and convinced of its significance. Review comments, however, must be evaluated and finally responded to with emotional neutrality. The first view of the negative comments makes the biggest impression. Fuller (1982) calls this Stage I: the onset of anxiety and panic. During this stage the investigator's attention is drawn to the comments viewed as the most serious criticisms and to those whose response will require the most effort.

Stage II according to Fuller can take the form of depression, shame, or anger. The potential investigator is besieged by doubts of his or her ability to think and to achieve success in a research program, shame about what others will say when they learn that the project has not been funded, and anger at the funding source for failing to perceive the value of the proposed project. This difficult situation is made more difficult because not all of the regular coping mechanisms developed for other professional criticism are useful. In this situation, however one responds, there is only one appropriate thing to do if the application is to be resubmitted: Each criticism must, after careful thought and consultation with colleagues about it, be addressed in writing, whether it is unfair, unjustified, or arises out of ignorance or misinformation.

INTERPRETING THE REVIEWERS' COMMENTS

Reading and interpreting reviewers' comments require experience and the art of reading between the lines. Funding source staff members usually compile comments from the original reviewers' statements. Sometimes comments of individuals can be apparent. Looking for areas of disagreement and overlap among the reviewers can lead to a better understanding of the review.

Do not be unduly encouraged by opening statements with positive comments. Remember, reviewers have gone through the same experiences that you are going through, and they do not wish to be harsh. Usually, reviewers will discuss their positive perception of the project, and perhaps specifically its value and uniqueness. Recognition of similarities between the reviewers' comments about your application and those you read while you were developing your project can help you adopt a positive attitude about the comments.

The level of critical comments and positive comments is reflected in the ranking of the application. Sometimes, however, there are very few, or very minor criticisms or negative comments and a poor ranking for the application. This kind of review usually represents a situation in which reviewers for some reason reacted negatively to the application even though their criticisms concerned minor points. In this situation, it is critical to contact the program project staff to determine how the negative impression arose, and whether there is a way to correct it in a revised application. It is not appropriate to contact members of the review group.

Selecting the Appropriate Response

Your first reaction to reviewers' comments might be that you did not get a fair review. After reading the reviewers' comments several times, you can view them with greater detachment and realism. Conversations with colleagues help promote detachment because these colleagues, more likely than not, have coped with similar reviews and have often succeeded in responding to them successfully and in getting funded subsequently. One of the decisions to be made is about the review process. If the review was unfair, then a rebuttal might be considered. If the review is appropriate, then the decision must be made about resubmitting or redesigning the idea as a new project.

Rebuttal Letter

It is possible to develop a rebuttal when it appears from the review comments that an error has been made during the assignment and application review. Contact the funding source to determine whether rebuttals are accepted and ask about the procedures for preparing a rebuttal. Ordinarily only written rebuttals are accepted.

The decision to write a rebuttal requesting corrective action is appropriate if there appears to be a serious error in the assignment of your application to a study section or in the process or substance of the application's review. However, the decision to write a rebuttal should be made only with thoughtful consultation with your collaborators and other colleagues. The rebuttal is usually addressed to the program staff, not to the reviewers. The advice that Reif-Lehrer (1989, p. 99) gives about writing a letter of rebuttal is that it should be "constructive and written in a positive tone . . . Intrusion of sarcasm, righteous indignation, and 'sour grapes' statements in a letter of rebuttal helps no one, least of all you! Under no circumstances should you attempt to contact individual Study Group members."

Letters of rebuttal do not always result in changed ranking, even if the application is rereviewed or reevaluated. Our advice is to think and think again about writing a rebuttal letter. In our opinion, the time and energy required to write this letter would be better used to revise the application or to prepare it for submission as a new application to the same or to another funding source.

Revise and Resubmit

The first thing to consider before making a decision about resubmission is whether project data collection is to occur in a window that will no longer exist 9 to 12 months in the future when the project would be funded. Clearly, there is no point in resubmitting the proposal if the planned window will be gone and you will be unable to create a new window of opportunity.

Second, determine whether resubmissions are acceptable to the selected funding source. Not all funding sources accept resubmissions, and some calls for applications are restricted to a single submission, such as the Requests for Applications (RFA) or Requests for Proposals (RFP) of NIH. If your funding source accepts resubmissions, check current research interests and the due dates for applications. Keep in mind that 6 to 9 months have passed since you last looked at this information. Some funding sources change their research interests on a regular basis, and application receipt dates are often changed to meet organizational needs.

Third, consider your application's ranking by the review group. Your decision to revise and resubmit must take the rank into account. We suggest you determine the funding cutoff from the program project staff in making this decision.

A Strategy for Developing Responses to Criticism

The process for responding to criticisms varies with the target of the criticism. Some of the reviewers' criticisms are easy to satisfy; others are difficult. The following are some suggestions for how to begin addressing the reviewers' comments.

Reread your application in light of the criticism. Many times criticisms can be met merely by rewording the trouble spot. This might mean tightening the language, deleting intrusive information, or reorganizing the information to more clearly guide the reviewers' thoughts.

Review the funding source's priorities. Perhaps your project is similar to the interests of the funding source, but the review group could not distinguish your project from what had already been funded or perceive how it would make a contribution to the knowledge domain of interest to them.

If you agree with the criticisms, rethink, rewrite, or redesign the troublesome section. It is advisable to use the criticisms as your guide in assessing the extent to which the project needs to be revised. This rewritten material must also be melded with the other parts of the proposal. Keep in mind that a resubmission might be read as a new application, and sometimes read by a different review group than read your original application.

After you are confident you understand the problems underlying the criticism, carefully write your responses to them, paying particular attention to detail. The next step is to ask a colleague not associated with the application to review the application, the reviewers' comments, and your proposed responses. Ask the colleague for candid remarks and criticisms. At this stage you want to be able to discuss negative comments, try out new solutions, and discover and correct communication problems before they get to the review group.

Very Poor Rank

Whatever the ranking system, a score that places your proposal at the poorest level is a serious recommendation from the review group that you should not revise and resubmit. However, this suggestion does not necessarily spring from correct conclusions on the part of the reviewers. A poor score could result from a review by an inappropriate review group or from misunderstandings about what the research was designed to accomplish. Perhaps the application included instrumentation, methodology, or programming not normally used.

A low score also arises from the review group's opinions that the application does not fall within the funding source's interests or mission. Although the latter instances are rare, because one of the early tasks for the PI is to determine whether the proposed research is within the mission statement of the funding source, they do happen. In this instance you may or may not get reviewer comments. If you do, look them over carefully for any assistance they can provide in strengthening your application before you submit it to another funding source.

A low score resulting from perceived serious flaws or insufficient value of the proposed project requires more thought and discussions with others who have submitted applications. We would like to stress that resubmitting an application that received a low score requires a great deal of work and the decision should receive sufficient consideration. Often, with major revision, an application takes a new direction or fills a different need. A decision not to revise and resubmit but to rethink the design and submit it as a new application is more often congruent with the ideas of the PI than a project directed to the reviewers' comments. Remember, do not feel unduly encouraged by positive review comments in opening statements. In the face of a very poor score, do not misconstrue these statements as encouragement and gloss over the specific criticisms outlined in the following paragraphs of the comments.

A Moderate to Good Rank

Applications that fall into this range can generally be improved. We suggest you do not significantly change the basic ideas or the project. Use the reviewers' comments for guidance on what to modify and voluntarily modify other aspects only when the integrity of the project is at risk. Revising and resubmitting applications within this range should be seriously considered.

An Excellent Rank

Very little can usually be done to improve an application that has received an excellent score. If significant improvement cannot be made, contact your funding source to determine what happens if you do not resubmit and you do not withdraw your application. Some funding sources leave applications in the system and evaluate them for funding in future funding cycles. This would be a good choice when no significant changes can be made. The problem with making small changes and resubmitting the application is that it may go to a new review group, or the review group membership may have changed and the score is vulnerable to reduction. This decision is best made with input from your collaborators and colleagues who have submitted applications. Of course, if your funding source does not permit applications to remain in the system, then there is no choice but to revise and resubmit.

THE REVISED APPLICATION

A revised application must meet the same high standards as the original application. Funding sources often require additional material outlining the changes that have been made in the document. For example, the PHS 398 application for revised applications includes an Introduction section limited to three pages (subject to the same type and page size constraints as the Research Plan). The instructions for the introduction are the following: "Summarize any substantial additions, deletions and changes that have been made. The Introduction must include responses to criticisms in the previous summary statement. Highlight these changes within the text of the Research Plan by appropriate bracketing, indenting, or change of typography. Do not underline or shade changes. Incorporate in the Progress Report/Preliminary Studies section any work done since the prior version was submitted. *A revised application will be returned if it does not address criticisms in the previous summary statement and/or an introduction is not included/and or substantial revisions are not clearly apparent*" (p. 20).

If you plan to resubmit an application, check the funding source policies. As is apparent from the above instructions in the PHS 398 packet, funding sources can have specific rules about how these applications should look, and they will return applications that do not meet their criteria. In general, your statement responding to the review group criticisms establishes that the application is revised, identifies extensive changes, corrects shortcomings of the original application, and clarifies issues to eliminate misunderstandings. We suggest that even if the funding source neither formally requires such a statement nor discourages it, it is beneficial to include the information in a statement or in a cover letter.

Responding to Criticism

Although you probably will not cease to experience emotions during the entire time you are preparing the resubmission, a neutral tone must be maintained in your replies to the criticisms. Sarcasm and veiled insults do not have a place. Begin the response to criticisms by expressing appreciation for the review group's effort and thoughtfulness in their review and written comments. State that the recommendations have been considered and followed for an improved application. State the criticisms verbatim, in the order in which they appear in the review comments, and respond to them one by one. Frequently the areas of criticism are those you have already thought about, so it is easy to respond in an even-handed way. This might include reorganizing material so that your logic becomes clearer. It might require additional information or an expanded discussion of your reasons for choosing what you have chosen. Reif-Lehrer (1989, p. 97) lists several possible sources of critical comments:

- Comments that represent the proposal inaccurately often result from unclear writing by the Principal Investigator.
- Criticisms about protocols, techniques, or data analysis often indicate the Principal Investigator didn't do enough homework.
- If the critique questions the ability of the Principal Investigator to carry out the proposed work, an appropriate collaborator may be in order.
- If the critique questions the choice of problem, ask yourself if the significance was poorly explained (rewrite)—OR—if the problem per se lacks merit (pick a new problem).

Respond to each criticism in some way. Criticisms might be a function of a reviewer misunderstanding or of not reading carefully. Remember, the burden of understanding is on your shoulders. Rewrite the sentence or section, being as clear and complete as you can be in addressing the area of misunderstanding.

Usually following the suggestions on the comment sheets is advisable. However, if a comment suggests a direction that you believe is not appropriate, include the information about the suggested direction and its consequences and explain why you will pursue the course you have chosen. The following is how one PI handled the situation in a revised application:

One alternative explanation suggested in the summary statement is that . . . may be in the low risk group. The current proposal acknowledges the possibility that effective . . . may only be a characteristic of certain individuals. . . . Current ongoing work in our laboratory is now addressing these issues. Additional studies are in progress to examine more precisely the distribution of . . . across various demographic boundaries. Until this issue is clarified, the original theory remains the driving force behind this systematic research program, and the theory will continue to be refined as additional data dictate. Alternative explanations will continue to be acknowledged, and the general approach in this systematic research program is to proceed with theory-driven research with consideration of multiple working hypotheses when the original theory becomes insufficient to explain existing data.

We are happy to report that the research was funded.

Depending upon the project development time and your funding source, it might be 3 months to a year since the application you are revising was last completed. This is sufficient time for changes to occur in an investigator's biographical sketch, in the institution's resources, and in the institution's policies and regulations. It is important, therefore, that each part of the application be reviewed and information updated when appropriate.

ACTION STRATEGIES

Getting Over the First Hurdle

Do not rush into reading and responding to the reviewer comments. Most PIs spend time thinking about the comments before responding. It will probably take some time before you can sit down and read the review comments from beginning to end in a relatively calm fashion. There is usually no point in hurrying into the revision mode. Revising an application too soon can be a total waste of time and effort. Also, do not forget your collaborators. They are going to be distressed by the fact that the application was not funded. Discussing the comments with them, as well as possible replies for resubmission, is important.

Recouping Losses

Discuss your application and the reviewer comments with colleagues who have had application experience and with those who know your project area. Meet with your collaborators to weigh the pros and cons of resubmitting.

Weaknesses must be strengthened, and the extent to which this is possible should be discussed with your collaborators.

REFERENCES

Fuller, E. O. (1982). The pink sheet syndrome. *Nursing Research, 31*(3), 185-186.

Reif-Lehrer, L. (1989). *Writing a successful grant application* (2nd ed.). Boston: Jones and Bartlett.

U.S. Department of Health and Human Services, Public Health Service. (1991). *Grant application form PHS 398* (p. 20). Washington, DC: U.S. Government Printing Office.

Index

About the Authors

Joanne B. Ries is Research Grant Facilitator and Departmental Research Director of the Department of Behavioral Science, College of Medicine, at the University of Kentucky. She received her Doctorate of Higher Education from the University of Kentucky in 1983, and a master's in Psychology from the University of Montana. She has been active in facilitating research in the Department of Behavioral Science for more than 20 years with concentration on research grant applications during the last decade. During this time, she has not only been involved in all phases of the application process, but has also been listening carefully to the questions, musings, and concerns of investigators. She has an inside perspective on application activities from brainstorming about research design and statistical approaches, editing for clarity and logic, counting the letters per inch, to negotiating the administrative maze.

She has been co-author of research articles and has edited research applications; has consulted with investigators in medicine, nursing, and the behavioral sciences; and has presented grant writing seminars.

Carl G. Leukefeld is Professor of Psychiatry and Director of the Drug and Alcohol Research Center at the University of Kentucky. He received his Doctorate of Social Work from the Catholic University of America in 1975 and his master's degree at the University of Michigan. Before going to the University of Kentucky, he was a commissioned officer in the U.S. Public Health Service, and for much of that time he was assigned to the National Institute on Drug Abuse in various clinical, management, and scientific capacities. He has given numerous presentations and has written articles focusing on treatment, criminal justice, prevention, and AIDS. His current research interests include the use of judicial sanctions, drug abuse treatment, the delivery of rural services, and the impact of HIV on the drug abuser.

He has co-edited 10 books. He is also an editor or a consulting editor for four professional journals and has served as a consultant to several international and national organizations including the Council on Europe, World Health Organization, U.S. Customs, U.S. Army, U.S. Navy, Administrative Office of the U.S. Courts, National Institute of Justice, National Institute of Corrections, American Probation and Parole Association, as well as state and local agencies.

He was first chairperson of the National Association of Social Workers, Health and Mental Health Commission. In 1991, he was elected to the National Academy of Practice in Social Work as a Distinguished Scholar. He was also selected as a Kentucky Colonel in 1991. He is the former chief health service officer of the U.S. Public Health Service and now resides in Lexington, Kentucky.

Lightning Source UK Ltd.
Milton Keynes UK
UKOW02f0614111114

241425UK00003B/123/A